The
BABEUF PLOT

BABEUF.

The

BABEUF PLOT

The Making of a Republican Legend

By
DAVID THOMSON, M.A., Ph.D.
FELLOW AND TUTOR OF SIDNEY SUSSEX COLLEGE
CAMBRIDGE

GREENWOOD PRESS, PUBLISHERS
WESTPORT, CONNECTICUT

Library of Congress Cataloging in Publication Data

Thomson, David, 1912-
   The Babeuf plot.

   Reprint of the 1947 ed. published by K. Paul,
Trench, Trubner, London.
   Bibliography: p.
   Includes index.
   1. Babeuf, Francois Noël, 1760-1797. 2. Social-
ism in France. I. Title.
DC187.8.T5 1975   944.04'092'4   75-27687
ISBN 0-8371-8466-5

First published in 1947 by Kegan Paul, Trench, Trubner
& Co., Ltd, London

Reprinted with the permission of Routledge & Kegan Paul, Ltd.

Reprinted in 1975 by Greenwood Press,
a division of Williamhouse-Regency Inc.

Library of Congress Catalog Card Number 75-27687

ISBN 0-8371-8466-5

Printed in the United States of America

TO

MY MOTHER AND FATHER

CONTENTS

PREFACE

THERE are three excuses, if any are needed, for the appearance at this time of a book about the Babeuf Plot and the legend it inspired.

First, and perhaps sufficient in itself, is the human interest of the story. It has few rivals among the many other picturesque and dramatic incidents of the French Revolution ; and it happened to be the final episode. The " Conspiracy of the Equals " has proved as ill-timed for its handling by historians as it was for its chances of success in 1796. The conventions of writing history demand that great events should begin and end in certain years. The French Revolution is regarded as ending in 1795 : the rise of Napoleon as dating from 1797, when he won his great Italian victories. The year 1796, in which the Babeuf Plot is perhaps the outstanding event, has dropped into one of the chinks of written history. The august *Cambridge Modern History* (Volume VIII) devotes exactly two pages to it, and Mr. J. M. Thompson, in the latest standard work on the French Revolution, ends with the death of Robespierre and ignores the Babeuf Plot. Similarly, in the study of political thought, the social ideas of the eighteenth-century *philosophes* such as Rousseau and of the nineteenth-century French socialists such as Saint-Simon and Louis Blanc are commonly treated in isolation ; yet the social ideas of Babeuf and his friends form the vital link between them.

Secondly, there is a curious contrast between the amount of attention paid to the legend of Babeuf in France and the unfamiliarity of Englishmen with even

ix

his name. The last English monograph—indeed the only full English monograph—devoted to Babeuf is that which the English Socialist Mr. E. B. Bax wrote in 1911 and called *The Last Episode of the French Revolution.* In the generation that has passed since it was written a mass of detailed research work has been carried out on the subject by French scholars. In France the attention paid—and still paid—to Babeuf and the legend of Babouvism is very considerable. At a time when Socialist and Communist forces are more important in France than ever before, it may be no bad thing that some knowledge of the movement which has been so venerated by Socialists and Communists in France should become more readily available in England.

Finally, the year 1947 is the one hundred and fiftieth anniversary of the death of Babeuf, and it is a kindly literary custom to pay some homage even to half-forgotten figures on such occasions.

The purpose of this little book is twofold. It aims, on the one hand, at telling the story of Babeuf's life and of the ill-fated conspiracy of which he became the centre, as clearly and accurately as possible. It attempts, on the other hand, to add some description and explanation of the republican legend which grew up during the nineteenth century linked with the name of Babeuf. The *mystique* of Babouvism has played a considerable but much neglected part in French political life. There is every temptation to interpret the events of 1796–7 in the light of this later legend. This I have steadily tried to avoid. If Babeuf is not interesting enough for his own sake, and if his ideas have no lasting significance in themselves, he is not worth hearing about at all. But the legend, though a different story and a separate accretion to the historical facts of the Babeuf Plot, has also a distinct importance and interest of its own. It casts some light on the meaning of republicanism and democracy in the Fourth French Republic.

I have to record my great gratitude to Miss Mary Southcombe for her constant help at every stage of preparing this book. Without that help, it would never have been written.

D. T.

Sidney Sussex College,
Cambridge.   1946.

Chapter I

APPRENTICESHIP OF A REVOLUTIONARY

THE legend of Babeuf begins with his birth. What is known about the circumstances of his birth and parentage is known in spite of the efforts of his father, himself and his son to obscure them for posterity. It seems that François-Noël Babeuf was in fact born at Saint-Quentin on Sunday, November 23, 1760, and was baptized the following day ; and that his parents were Claude Babeuf and Marie Catherine Anceret. His father founded the legend that he had been born on Christmas night, 1760, at " about the same time as our Redeemer ", and that he had been christened Noël because of the striking resemblance of his mother's condition to that of an earlier Mary—" without fire, linen or food ", and without even the help of neighbours, who were all at Mass. Babeuf also spread the story that they were so poverty-stricken that his father had to baptize the children himself, because the priests would not officiate without money—a story disproved by the survival of the actual certificate of baptism. It seems true, however, that his cradle was " a worm-eaten bread-box ", affording cramped conditions which he later blamed for his own smallness of stature.

His father, Claude Babeuf, was evidently a man of considerable character and education, and of even greater imagination. He had had a career in the French and Austrian armies—distinguished enough, for he became a Major, but less distinguished than he liked to make out. In 1738 he had deserted from his cavalry regiment, fled from France, and returned only in 1755 when Louis XV granted him a pardon for his desertion. He secured a job in the tax-farming business—collecting the famous *gabelle*, or salt-tax ; and this job he held when François-Noël was born in 1760. The certificate of baptism describes the father as *employé des fermes du roy au foubourg St. Martin de la ville de St. Quentin*. Earlier that year, at the age of forty-eight, Claude had married the girl of twenty who was in due course to become the mother not only of the famous François-Noël, but also of numerous other progeny. The family was prolific—in Babeuf's own phrase, " in growing proportion to its profound distress ". Claude, for reasons unknown, lost his government post for a time and was reduced to working as a navvy on the military fortifications at Saint-Quentin ; and whatever had been the family fortunes in 1760, they were soon reduced to nothing with an ever-growing family to keep on a navvy's wages. The five children could not be sent to school, and so far as they were educated at all they were educated by the gallant Major.

From him the eldest son, at least, learnt the rudiments of mathematics, Latin and German—enough, in short, for him to aid the family income at the age of sixteen by becoming junior clerk and apprentice to a *commissaire à terrier*. This post, peculiar to the semi-feudal conditions of the *ancien régime* in France, requires some explanation ; for it was strongly to colour the impressionable youth's early career and outlook.

One function of the *commissaire à terrier* was land-surveying, and the work involved considerable mathematical and technical knowledge of surveying. Another, more important and lucrative function was that of keeping a full and detailed account of the property on an estate ; and property then included a tangle of feudal rights and privileges as well as material goods. The successful *commissaire* was therefore primarily something of an accountant and an archivist, expert in understanding and interpreting complex legal records. His most valuable— and to his employer most valued—duty was to safeguard the mass of petty rights and exact the full quota of dues and services from the tenants of the estate. It is an odd occupation in which to find the future champion of doctrinaire equality and the advocate of communism in all property ; but in it lies one clue to the fervent fanaticism of the would-be founder of the " Republic of Equals ". His revulsion against his distasteful oppressive duties bred fanaticism.

By 1777 he was employed as a domestic servant by M. de Bracquemont, Seigneur de Damery, near the town of Roye. This fact, too, his son was later to deny, in a misguided effort to show that his father never owed anything to noble patronage. But the boy was already helping to keep his brother and sisters, and when his father died in 1781 he had to assume responsibility for keeping his mother as well. It is known from a letter of François-Noël to his father, dated May 26, 1780, that he was then employed by a M. Hullin of Flixecourt, at a salary of three livres per month after his first year's (unpaid) employment. In 1782 he married a housemaid of the Countess de Bracquemont, Marie-Anne-Victoire Langlet, daughter of Antoine Langlet ; she was nearly four years older than Babeuf.

Her son was later to exalt her own position, claiming that she was " the friend of a noble lady who had taken her out of a convent in order to have her company ". A sense of the dramatic and colourful was always stronger with all three generations of Babeufs than a sense of the strictly accurate. She was in any case practically illiterate, and of very poor parentage. The following year, with one daughter already arrived, François-Noël and his wife were living at Roye, a small town in Picardy, and he was acting as a *commissaire à terrier* in his own right.   He, like his father, raised a larger family than he could support.   Six more children were born, of whom only three survived childhood.   The eldest son, Robert, later called Émile, was born in 1785 ; he was to play a part in the growth of the legend of Babouvism.

So François-Noël, a young married man of twenty-five in 1785, with at least a moderately lucrative employment, could claim to have raised himself from extreme poverty by his own abilities and exertions.   So far as he was " made " at twenty-five, he was self-made.   Industrious, studious, persistent, he had qualified himself for a post which held considerable possibilities.   But it had been achieved only against heavy odds, and at the expense of ten years of sweated labour.   Perhaps this explains his later contention that education had become " a kind of property ", and that it should either be provided for all equally, or denied to all equally.

The years 1785–8 brought a new phase in his life.   He entered into a long and arduous philosophical correspondence with Dubois de Fosseux, secretary of the *Académie royale des belles-lettres d'Arras*.   It was one of many such literary and scientific societies which sprang up in most important French towns in the age of " enlightenment ".   One of their functions was to organize competitions for prize essays providing solutions to specific problems.   It was in such a competition run by the Academy of Dijon in 1750 that Jean-Jacques Rousseau won the prize for his discourse on the subject :   " Has the restoration of the arts and sciences had a purifying effect upon morals ? "   The question posed at Arras a generation later was more mundane, but it attracted the young surveyor just as much as the previous subject had attracted the moralist Rousseau.   It was :

Is it of advantage to reduce the number of roads in the territory of the villages in the province of Artois, and to make those that remain broad enough to be planted with trees ? In the event of an affirmative answer, indicate how such a scheme should be carried out.

It is doubtful whether the summary essay submitted by Babeuf would have won the prize ; in any case he disqualified himself by late entry and by not preserving that anonymity of authorship which the terms of the competition required. It began, however, the long personal correspondence with the secretary of the Academy, Dubois, in the course of which Babeuf's ideas on politics and economics were to take some shape.

It was from the first an unequal correspondence. Dubois was forty-three and already a figure of provincial importance. Babeuf was but twenty-five, and hitherto virtually unknown. But Dubois came more and more to seek Babeuf's views and comments on a vast variety of subjects, many of which had been raised by members of the Academy of Arras. It provided immense mental stimulus to the young man. It brought him into direct contact with the fermenting ideas of the enlightenment which were so soon to bear fruit in the early phases of the great Revolution.

At first Babeuf was clearly pleased and immensely flattered by the confidences and attentions of so eminent a man of culture. He is found confiding in Dubois that he hopes to bring up his eldest son, Robert, in the educational principles expounded by Rousseau—even re-christening him privately Émile, in homage to the work of Jean-Jacques. In March 1787 he sent Dubois a copy of a booklet on *La Constitution du Corps-militaire*, which he said had been written by a friend and for which he sought publicity. Dubois proffered polite commendation on the book, but considered it too dangerously " against the Government " to be sponsored and published. It had probably been written by Babeuf himself. In the same month, in response to requests for subjects of discussion, he suggested one which has some significance as an indication of how his ideas were shaping. It ran thus :

> Given all present knowledge, what would be the state of a people whose social institutions were such that there would prevail among its individual members, without any distinctions, the most perfect equality ; that the soil they would live on belonged to no one but to all ; that everything would be held in common, including the product of every kind of industry ? Would such institutions be authorized by natural law ? Would it be possible for this society to survive ? And, further, would there be practicable means of securing absolutely equal distribution ?

Dubois, in return, propounded the possible synopsis of a book with the characteristically optimistic eighteenth-century title, *Le Changement du monde entier*. The practical purpose was to set out devices and arrangements whereby " all citizens who are in need, or who enjoy only a modest fortune, may—together with their wives and children—be in future well nourished, clothed, lighted and warmed, receive a perfect education, and enjoy, by means of honest labour, each according to his (or her) strength, abilities, sex, age, talent, trade or profession, much more ease, liberty, justice, comfort and advantage than at present."

Here were echoes from several of the earlier *philosophe* writers, who had sown the first seeds of utopian socialism in France ; echoes of Rousseau's discourse on " What is the origin of inequality among men, and is it authorized by natural law ? " (1753–5) ; echoes of Morelly's *Code*

de la Nature (1755) ; echoes of the Abbé Mably's *De la
Législation* (1776). Many crudely egalitarian and communistic ideas were in the air in the second half of the
eighteenth century. What is perhaps remarkable is that
such ideas, when propounded by Dubois, seemed to hold
little attraction for Babeuf. He dubbed the author of the
proposed book—who was doubtless Dubois himself—" a
mere dreamer ". Here, perhaps, is an early hint of the
role which Babeuf was to play in the development of communist ideas. He already had no use for ideas which were
in the clouds : he wanted them to be reduced to concrete
proposals before they attracted him. He was to become,
in short, the essential bridge between the airy and vague
utopian communism of the eighteenth-century *philosophes*
and the less utopian socialists of the nineteenth century—
Fourier, Saint-Simon, Proudhon and Louis Blanc ; and
he was to be adopted as the precursor of the more scientific
communism of Marx. From Morelly he had already
learnt a principle which he was to transmit to modern
communism : " from each according to his ability, to
each according to his needs ". And that, in a wider sense
than Morelly or Babeuf conceived it, is the basic notion
of all modern socialistic and communistic legislation, and
of the modern " social-service " State.

The prolific correspondence of Dubois began to prove
too much for the hard-working youth with a family to
keep (indeed two families, since he still supported his
mother and sisters). By March 1788, after more than
two years of it, Dubois complains that Babeuf is neglecting
to return certain literary pieces he has sent, and Babeuf's
replies were evidently getting shorter and shorter, with
longer intervals between them. He begged Dubois to
remember that he had other work to do, a family to feed,
and that his knowledge was not encyclopædic. This odd
interlude in his life, during which he had been able to

discuss with a cultured friend an amazing range of topics covering ⸱inoculation, magnetism, the organization of agriculture, and sugar-manufacture, as well as politics and economics, had widened and variegated his interests and ideas without doing much to harden them.   There are a few signs of the future doctrinaire revolutionary, and some of the egalitarian communist.   But there is little, beyond his obvious affection for the notions of Morelly and Rousseau, to show in what direction his life was to be spent.

The next phase—of more creative literary and journalistic activity—was to bring that hardening of ideas which he had hitherto lacked.   It coincided with several bitter experiences in his professional career ;   and it is this coincidence of mental development and actual experience which helps to explain the twist given to his whole life.

The years 1788–92, which brought the entry of Babeuf into active political journalism and serious reverses in his private fortunes, coincided, too, with the outbreak of the great Revolution.   The course of his own life seemed to chime with the course of French history ;   which gives it a dramatic unity, and even a symbolism, that have proved particularly potent in the growth of the legend of Babouvism.

Until 1788 his own literary productions had been ill-fated.   His prize essay had been disqualified ;   his *Constitution du Corps-militaire* (if it was indeed his) had been rejected as too dangerous ;   his proposed work on *l'Archiviste-Terriste*, dealing with his professional work and problems, found no governmental support and remained in manuscript.   In 1786 he had published a brochure entitled *Mémoire pour les Propriétaires de Terres et de Seigneuries, ou Idées sur la manutention des Fiefs*, which dealt with the same problems ;   and in the same year a *Discours sur les causes des désordres qui se remarquent trop souvent dans les titres des Seigneuries.*   In the latter he incorporated political reflections on the political inertia of the majority of men.

> The majority is always on the side of routine and immobility, so much is it unenlightened, encrusted, apathetic ;   and, amongst this majority, there are also enlightened men who are no less obstinate than the rest in their inertia.   Some reject progress because it will injure their interests, others because it means a new way of behaving or of living.   This is why excellent inventions, useful methods and processes, pass by unnoticed ;   this is why progress remains in the realm of mere theory which people are wary of examining.   Those who do not want to move forward are the enemies of those who do, and unhappily it is the mass which persists stubbornly in never budging at all.

But all this writing was primarily technical, and little calculated to appeal to a wide public.

It was the Revolution which stimulated him to more popular journalism.   In 1789, when the localities began to draw up those *Cahiers,* or statements of grievances, which were to be presented to the new Estates-General, he took an active part in preparing the *Cahier* of Roye in Picardy.   He tried without success to get included a demand for the abolition of feudal tenures and the substitution of a single tax, irrespective of class, for the mass of existing imposts.   He was in Paris soon after the Bastille fell on July 14, and during the epidemic of local attacks on the castles of the nobility he helped to burn the seignorial archives at Roye.   Here is the real turning-point in his life.   The professional archivist engaged in destroying the materials of his own livelihood had clearly cut adrift from his own past and his own profession.   He had become

B*

a revolutionary ; but he had not yet become a professional revolutionary.

The main reasons for this break lie in his own experiences. In 1787, in the course of his work, he had been engaged by the Comte de Castéja, Marshal of the camps and armies of the King. The Count had picked a quarrel with him over a petty business of whether he should dine with the Count's other employees, and wrote a haughty, stinging letter of rebuke. Babeuf replied with some dignity, but the taunt plainly embittered him. It was typical of the behaviour of the nobles towards the lower-middle-class folk whom they employed ; an attitude made all the more intolerable by the frequent tendency of the same nobles to cheat their employees out of their just wages whenever possible, as Babeuf was soon to discover.

He was building up a good practice among the nobility and clergy of the locality, though the work of pursuing the poor was becoming increasingly distasteful to him. The Prior of Saint Taurin engaged him on work which took six months and resulted in considerable increase of the Prior's revenue ; but he haggled about the costs, and only after threats of litigation was a fee agreed between them. The Marquis of Soyecourt likewise engaged his services, but when the bill for 12,000 livres was presented by Babeuf, the noble Marquis offered only 100 louis (i.e. 2,400 livres). Incapable of entering upon a costly lawsuit with so powerful a man, Babeuf was forced to accept this meagre reward. The Abbé de Broglie also owed him considerable fees. All this ruined him financially, and brought great hardship to his family. At the end of 1787 he had to move to a poorer working-class district of Roye. Such incidents embittered him, and do much to explain the hardening of his feelings towards the privileged classes. Exasperation and bitterness were his mood when the

Bastille fell, giving the cue for the general looting and burning of the seignorial *château* all over France.

The social background and experience of Babeuf was, it must be remembered, quite typical of the majority of men of his class and upbringing. It was common for one child in four to die before it was ten. Hunger, poverty and distress were the common lot of the working and lower middle classes in the *ancien régime*. Extortionate and dishonest landowners, lay or ecclesiastical, were all too common. Bad harvests in 1787 and 1788 increased the distress of all but the privileged ; and in the winter of 1788, which saw Babeuf's personal fortunes at their lowest ebb since his early youth, prices rocketed in France. " The whole countryside ", writes J. M. Thompson, " lived in a state of dull resentment against feudalism and privilege, which might at any time break out into a local *jacquerie* or *bacchanale*." The summoning of the Estates-General in the spring of 1789 raised hopes of more bread, as well as of social and political reforms. There were food riots even before the Bastille fell, but that dramatic event turned them into the political risings of the summer of 1789. All over France events took place like those at Roye : estate-owners were attacked, cellars and larders were looted, and the seignorial archives of legal documents —the source of countless superstitious fears and of age-long oppression—were dragged out and burned. It was Babeuf's whole profession, as well as the materials on which it worked, that went up in flames in the great *jacquerie* of 1789. He became a journalist partly because he wanted to, but partly, too, because he had to. Combined with the great surrender of noble privileges on August 4, these events turned him into a man whose only remaining useful skill was his pen ; they also offered, at last, an opportunity for urging and securing some of those reforms in economic and social life which he had long cherished. France was thrown into the melting-pot, and he might do something to determine what should come out of it. So he began to write.

He was in Paris from July to October 1789 : four decisive months in his own career, as well as in the history of his country. His personal losses and mood put him in tune with the seething Paris populace in which he lived. Opposed to the efforts of Mirabeau to find some working compromise between King and people which would yield a constitutional monarchy, he wrote a pamphlet called *La nouvelle distinction des Ordres, par M. de Mirabeau.* He joined with an old acquaintance, Audiffred, in producing in 1789 the *Cadastre perpétuel*—a sort of comprehensive land-register, showing the territorial divisions and conditions of land tenure throughout France. It was dedicated to the National Assembly. This, his son was later to claim, " fixed the method for the division of the *départements*, but brought nothing to its author ". Were this so, Babeuf would certainly have left his mark on modern France. But it was largely ignored and hardly sold at all, and there is no evidence for the claim. In collaboration with a printer friend at Noyon he founded a journal called *Le Correspondent Picard,* of which forty numbers appeared. It brought him, he declared, two hundred law-suits in six months—from which the character and spirit of the journal can be judged. He attacked the franchise of 1789, suggesting that in place of the three orders there were now four—" the Pennies, Shillings, Crowns, and Sovereigns ". It also brought him a short term of imprisonment, from which he was released in time to take part in the Bastille celebrations of 1790—the first anniversary of the great event. But it did not bring him as much money as notoriety, and his family still lived in poverty at Roye. He had now made some name for himself, however, as a demagogue and revolutionary and was committed to pressing the Revolution far beyond the stage of constitutional monarchy visualized by Mirabeau.

From 1789 until 1792, his residence in Roye amid working-class folk provided a certain apprenticeship in local politics and in the art of the popular agitator and demagogue. It offers, too, some sidelight on the working of the Revolution, in its early stages, in the provinces. The course of the French Revolution has been studied too exclusively from a Parisian point of view, and the tendency of most modern research in France has been to emphasize the relative slowness and the wide diversity of its progress in the provinces. The experience of Babeuf in Roye, offering one specific example of this aspect of the Revolution, acquires special interest.

The little township of Roye, famous in France for its remarkably high annual consumption of brandy, numbered some 3,000 souls. The *cabaretiers* of Roye were therefore an important and prosperous section of the little community.[1] In 1789 these inn-keepers employed Babeuf to promote their interests, and he was accused of fomenting agitation when the inhabitants of the town refused to pay local imposts. He became identified with disorderly popular movements in the eyes of even the revolutionary government. In 1790 he was elected, by fifteen votes, as member of the municipal council at Roye, but by the end of the year was ejected and declared ineligible under Government pressure. When a dispute arose between the *commune* and the monks of Amiens, who owned the big wood near Roye (the villagers had taken the law into their own hands, claimed the wood as communal property, and proceeded to cut down the trees), Babeuf was elected a commissioner for his district, with

[1] Marcel Marion, in his valuable *Dictionnaire des Institutions de la France aux XVIIe et XVIIIe siècles*, writes : Il y avait trois sortes de cabarets : ceux à pot et à pinte, c'est-à-dire ne vendant qu'à boire ; ceux à pot et assiette, vendant aussi à manger ; et ceux qui en outre logeaient.

the duty of investigating and determining the rights of the *commune*. After a violent scene in which the Mayor was coerced, Babeuf was arrested on the orders of the Government. In these years he clearly drifted into the ranks of the more active, discontented, left-wing, working-class elements, getting frequently into trouble with the authorities for his activities.

In a letter written on August 20, 1791, Babeuf made this significant complaint :

> There is a powerful horde of detractors who look upon me as one of the greatest menaces to the mass of abuses on which they and their like continue to fatten themselves. This class of parasites on society never miss a chance to launch attacks against me. . . . They have treacherously struck at all my sources of income, diminishing them one by one, inciting and encouraging my debtors not to pay me, my creditors to pursue me, persuading those who had commissioned my services to withdraw their commission.

Misfortune and harsh treatment were evidently inducing a sort of persecution-complex in Babeuf. He believed the interests threatened by his political activities to be conspiring against his person ; and the next step was to meet conspiracy with counter-conspiracy. He made, at the same time, the confession :

> Politics, and meditation on the true principles of laws and of their execution, hold so irresistible an attraction for me that I am inclined to think that there lies my true vocation.

He was drawn into politics and popular agitation almost to his own surprise.

In 1792 he secured the post of administrator and

archivist of the department of the Somme, which led him to settle in Amiens for a time. There he fell foul of the local Representative, André Dumonge, and the quarrel between them became so acute that Babeuf was forced to leave and get a similar post in the district of Montdidier. There in turn he incurred great hostility from the president of the district, an extreme royalist and an aristocrat, who accused him of forgery in his work. Babeuf, he alleged, had substituted one name for another in an act of sale of one of the national lands, recently taken from the Church. Though probably partly an oversight,[1] the error was difficult to defend in a law court, and Babeuf decided not to face trial. He fled to Paris, where he undertook certain literary work for an American adventurer named Fournier. Early in 1794 he secured another of those minor *fonctionnaire* posts with which his career had started : this time as secretary in the *Bureau des Subsistances* in Paris, under the Paris Commune. Discovering in this municipal department a great deal of peculation and leakage in accounts, he came to the conclusion that the authorities were planning an artificial famine and denounced them in public. This raised up against him many more influential enemies, who helped to secure his arrest by the Montdidier authorities on the old charge of forgery. In July 1794 the court unanimously declared that the charge was not proven, and his honour was vindicated. There is little doubt that it was a vindictive charge. But the persistent way in which Babeuf made enemies wherever he went, and the spite with which his enemies pursued him, are signs that his nature was somewhat quarrelsome. For the moment, then, he was again without a job, and the Revolution had reached another great turning-point.

---

[1] Cf. the detailed, if somewhat hostile, study by Abel Patoux : *Le Faux de Gracchus Babeuf.* (1913.) Certainly Babeuf derived no personal advantage from the incident, and his share seems to have been a minor one.

In the very month of Babeuf's acquittal, Robespierre fell and the Reign of Terror neared its end.

Babeuf returned to Paris, to his post in the *Commission des Subsistances*, and started his *Journal de la Liberté de la Presse* in which he attacked Robespierre and the Commune. He got on to good terms with the leaders of the Thermidorian reaction—especially with Tallien and Fouché—and embarked on public speaking. " Gracchus" Babeuf—as he now called himself—was finding his *métier* at last. He issued a pamphlet called *Du système de dépopulation ou la vie et les crimes de Carrier*. Like the *Journal* it attacked the Jacobins and levied against them the fantastic charge of deliberate depopulation. Robespierre, Barère and the former members of the Committee of Public Safety came in for direct personal abuse. Within a month or two the offensive was turned against the leaders of Thermidor themselves, and by October the Committee of General Security took action against the paper and its editor. Babeuf went into hiding and published the journal under a new and significant title—the *Tribun du Peuple*. The police sought in vain for Babeuf, but succeeded only in arresting the distributors of the journal. He was evidently extremely ingenious in his technique of clandestine printing and publishing. Tallien, his former friend, was attacked in the paper, and it was he who was eventually instrumental in securing Babeuf's arrest. He was seized on February 12, 1795. Even from prison he smuggled out a manifesto from " Babeuf, the Tribune of the People, to his Fellow Citizens ". He was moved from Paris to a prison in Arras. In prison he found the congenial company necessary for the final formulation and elaboration of his principles of communism. Like many another revolutionary creed, Babouvism was born in prison.

His companions in Arras prison were Lebois, editor of

Le journal de l'égalité ;   Taffoureau, who was probably a former friend from the days of the *Correspondent Picard* ; and Cochet, a colleague of Taffoureau's.   They were joined by various other people who found themselves thrown into prison during the factious squabbles between Thermidorians and *Sansculottes* ;   particularly by Charles Germain, who was to remain a colleague of Babeuf during the Conspiracy.   In September 1795 Babeuf and Germain were transferred back to Paris where they made the acquaintance of Buonarroti.   All three were soon released on an amnesty proclaimed by the National Convention at its closing session.   Launched from prison on the turbulent world of the Directory, after seven months in prison, the journalist had become an experienced conspirator, with a fervent faith in his own doctrines of equality.   He had become, at last, a professional revolutionary.

The nature of these doctrines, and of the plot by which Babeuf and his friends hoped to put them into practice, will be considered later.   It remains to review the curious process by which the penniless boy of 1776 had been turned into the penniless conspirator of 1795.   It is a process of successive hardships and failures, of honest industry frustrated and recurrent persecution.   In family relationships he had proved himself a devoted son and a loyal husband and father.   Despite almost constant poverty, broken only by periods of complete destitution, his family life seems to have remained harmonious and even happy. In August 1789 he was writing pitiful letters to his wife, affectionate and apologetic, about his plans for earning more money.   He inspired, in both wife and eldest son, unflinching devotion and hero-worship.   In the letter he wrote, the night before his execution, to his wife and children, he declared :

Your love for me has brought you hither, in spite

of all the obstacles of our misery. You have supported yourself here in the midst of difficulties and privations. Your constancy has made you follow all the proceedings of this long, cruel trial of which, like myself, you have drunk the bitter cup. . . . I hope that you will believe I have loved you all very much. I could conceive of no other way of making you happy than through the common welfare. I have failed : I am sacrificed ; it is for you also that I die. . . ."

His domestic relations seem, in every detail, to have been completely unblemished.

There runs through his whole life a constant thread of passionate sincerity and integrity of purpose. His ideas might change—certainly his judgment of political leaders like Robespierre changed abruptly and diametrically—but he was never a humbug. That he was quarrelsome and often tactless is plain enough ; that too derived from his sincerity. The only streak in his character which made him deviate from the truth as he saw it was his inveterate love of the dramatic, not to say the theatrical, which he doubtless inherited partly from his father. He could not resist dramatizing his own life and deeds, and the demands of dramatic unity sometimes conflicted with the literal truth. This propensity, combined with the similar tendencies of his father and his son, have shrouded his earlier life in stories many of which are undoubtedly apocryphal. The most famous is that which made the Emperor Joseph II of Austria, most doctrinaire of all eighteenth-century " Enlightened Despots ", seek to adopt Babeuf as a *protégé*. Claude Babeuf, the story runs, had, during his exploits as a Major in the army of Maria Theresa, been appointed tutor to the Empress's children. In after years the Emperor Joseph II happened to be passing through Picardy and came across the son of his former tutor. He immediately offered him the highest employment at the Court of Vienna. But François-Noël's democratic principles were even then so strong that he resolutely declined. Incurably romantic, Babeuf clung to this story despite all its improbabilities and obvious discrepancies with his own beliefs at that time. It was this sense of the dramatic, given free rein at his own trial and execution, which laid the basis for the *mystique* of the Babouvist legend.

The evolution of the *fonctionnaire* and technician into the demagogue and the conspirator was primarily due to two factors in constant interaction. On the one hand, the thoughtful, romantic, idealistic and very earnest young man was confronted with the most intimate experience of the harshness, injustices and distress of the *ancien régime.* Imbued with the optimistic progressive ideas of the *philosophes*, his mental and spiritual revulsion was bound to be extremely violent. On the other hand, the personal sense of frustration and persecution which came from repeated experience of the thanklessness, treachery and vindictiveness of those who felt their interests threatened, struck iron into his soul. His attitude to the well-to-do was not unmixed with envy, as befitted the affectionate father of hungry children. Amid the turbulence of the years of revolution, his personal misfortunes merged into the general upheaval : one was a microcosm of the other, and could be overcome only in the completion of the Revolution, its continuation into that fraternal " Republic of Equals " without rich or poor. To effect this completion of the Revolution, he conceived, was the mission of his life. He was persistently " against the Government ", whether it were Bourbon Monarchy, Mirabeau moderates, Girondins, Jacobins or Thermidorians, because all these were but obstacles to the final consummation of the original ideals of " Liberty, Equality, Fraternity ".

A modern psychologist would doubtless describe Babeuf as a paranoiac. According to the admittedly dubious evidence of one of his colleagues who later betrayed him, he was wont to work himself into a frenzy of excitement before he could write his inflammatory, rhetorical outbursts. He would pace nervously up and down the room, walking faster and faster until his eyes blazed and he snarled phrases from clenched teeth. After kicking the furniture and emitting cries of *Aux armes ! L'insurrection !* he would seize a pen and write furiously until he was bathed in sweat and his whole body trembled as if in a frenzy. However highly coloured may be this description of an enemy, it may be compared with Babeuf's own constant plea during his trial that he could not improvise. He was throughout the long ordeal careful to equip himself with elaborately prepared speeches, and when his judges urged him to be briefer and to cease exhausting them by reading from hundreds of pages of script, he accused them of trying to stifle his defence because they knew he could not speak extempore. Under the stress of great excitement during the trial, however, he proved himself capable of eloquent outbursts, exactly similar to his prepared harangues. Certainly he was a fanatical ideologue, convinced throughout of his own impeccable sincerity of purpose. That he had magnetic powers of leadership and a flair for demagogy is clear enough. All these qualities found outlet in the part he played in the plot which bears his name.

CHAPTER II

CRAFTSMANSHIP OF A REVOLUTIONARY

THERE were reasons enough for discontent in France of 1795. The excesses of the Terror and France's efforts in three years of strenuous foreign war had left her exhausted. The aftermath was deep social distress. True, the war had not proved disastrous, in spite of the coalitions formed by Mr. Pitt of England, and the subsidies with which he fed France's continental enemies. France as a nation was no longer in danger : her frontiers were safe. But the Constitution of the Year III (1795) adopted by the Convention created a more oligarchical form of government. Universal suffrage, chief tenet of the Jacobins, was abolished and a high property qualification was required of all voters. The effective—if not often very effective—government was the Directory of Five, of whom none save Carnot, the " organizer of victories ", inspired any confidence. The social upheaval of the Terror and the Thermidorian reaction were throwing up a powerful class of *nouveaux riches*—upstart " aristocrats " even more insufferable than their more elegant and refined predecessors of the *ancien régime*. The reckless issue of *assignats* in 1794–5 had brought ruin to the bulk of the middle classes and to all with fixed incomes who had hitherto profited by the abolition of feudal privileges. The only gainers from the inflation were, as always, those who had accumulated new landed estates and the financial speculators (*agioteurs*). Barras, one of the five Directors, had acquired five estates and several mistresses. Men such as Merlin de Thionville and Legendre—men of power and influence in the new *régime*—had lavishly feathered their own nests from the so-called " national " lands taken from the Church and the old nobility.

In Paris, and in other big towns, the economic situation was desperate. If the war had been successful, it seemed nowhere near its end. Supplies and transport were precarious, and even available supplies sold at prohibitive prices for all save the very wealthy. The gulf between rich and poor became more than ever conspicuous, for there were the new poor as well as the new rich. The forces of order and security were unreliable. The armies —even when fighting mostly on foreign soil—were ragged and ill cared for. The *gendarmerie* were prone to desertion, the police mutinous. The administration worked mainly because it afforded sufficient openings for peculation. Disorder was rampant in the unpatrolled streets and highways, and plots were in the air.

The Jacobins—now outcasts even when still alive—had plainly failed. The Terror had overshot the mark. But already, in these circumstances, men were beginning to look back to 1793 as a golden age of democracy. The cry of " Bread and the Constitution of 1793 "—so often to be raised again in the course of the nineteenth century —was first raised in 1795. The time was ripe for a fresh appeal to the mass of the people : an appeal for return to the original, impeccable, soul-stirring principles of 1793. Perhaps the time was even over-ripe, for in the provinces inertia was setting in. But whence could such an appeal come ? It came, in fact, from Babeuf.

In October 1795 was founded a political society with the aim of seeking economic equality as well as political equality, in defiance of the new Constitution. It amalgamated with a similar new revolutionary society of Parisians, and the merger-society—called the Society of the Panthéon—formed a club which met in the crypt of the Convent of Sainte Géneviève. Many disgruntled Jacobins adhered to the new club. The circulation amongst its members of Babeuf's paper the *Tribun* prepared the way for his leadership in the conspiracy. The club met at night to read and discuss his articles. It was in October (*Vendémiaire*) that the last great royalist insurrection had been crushed by Bonaparte, and the Directory hoped by some toleration of such Jacobin clubs to preserve reliable allies against further royalist risings. One of the society, Buonarroti, who became the chief perpetuator of Babouvism in the nineteenth century, has left a vivid description of their meetings in the crypt.

> The flicker of torches, the hollow echo of voices, and the attitudes of the members sitting or standing on the ground, leaning against the pillars, impressed everyone with the grandeur and danger of the whole enterprise, as well as the courage and prudence that it called for.

It was a curious hybrid of secret society and political party, and seems to have taken some considerable time to make up its mind what technique of organization was more appropriate. The result was that to a society admittedly insurrectionist in purpose were admitted many members whose reliability was little scrutinized—an elementary but highly dangerous weakness of any new political movement, as they were to learn to their cost. Buonarroti claims that it soon had two thousand members, but they appear to have been split between a left and a right wing : between the egalitarian followers of Babeuf and the former Jacobins. It was the inevitable cleavage in all the extreme revolutionary societies, and may be compared in some respects with the split between Mensheviks and Bolsheviks within the Social Democratic party a century later. Nor was the Society of the Panthéon the only such group in Paris at that time :

it was only one among many and would have sunk into the same oblivion as the rest but for the conspiracy which was to grow out of it in the following year.

At the beginning of 1796 the Directory decided to take action against the *Tribun* and its authors. Babeuf narrowly escaped arrest by the simple device of dodging the official sent to arrest him and running down the street faster than his pursuer. His wife was arrested instead—an act of victimization which brought the indignation of the Panthéonists to fever pitch. It won Babeuf active sympathy from many who had hitherto looked at him askance for his earlier support of the Thermidorians, and changed the temper of the Society, which had until then been moderated by its more cautious members. A few weeks later the *Tribun du Peuple* finally went out of publication, with the lament " All is finished. . . . It is no longer permitted to repeat that we live under the rule of the most abominable tyrants." All was indeed finished, historically, in the sense that the rule of the *nouveaux riches*, soon to find an even more stalwart champion in Bonaparte than in the Directory, was now firmly established. But all was far from finished for Babeuf. The most potent force in the legend of Babeuf was about to begin.

A fortnight after the attack on the *Tribun*, the Directory ordered the dissolution of the Society of the Panthéon and the closure of its meeting-place. At the end of February General Bonaparte came in person and seized the keys, and the convent which had come to be known in polite circles and to the police as " the Cave of Brigands " was securely shut. Throughout Paris the other revolutionary clubs and public meetings were suppressed. To the smouldering mood of desperation—the *assignats* were still falling calamitously—was added a new gust of persecution and repression which served to fan political debate into active conspiracy.

In the middle of March Charles Germain, distressed by the dissensions, wrote to Babeuf urging him to assume leadership and unite with a firm hand the diverse elements in the movement.   It was Babeuf who founded the *Comité insurrecteur*, the secret inner committee which planned the insurrection, and intrigued to weaken all rival committees. It consisted of six men, chief of whom were Babeuf, Darthé and Buonarroti.   The other three were Maréchal, Debon and Le Pelletier.   Augustin Alexandre Darthé, a native of the Pas-de-Calais, had taken part in the storming of the Bastille and had been a member of the directing body of that *département* in the earlier years of the Revolution.   A supporter of Robespierre, he became public prosecutor in the revolutionary tribunals at Arras and Cambrai.   He remained throughout the staunchest personal ally of Babeuf, and died with him on the scaffold.   Philippe Buonarroti, destined to play the major part in the transmission of Babouvism as a legend, had been born in Pisa in 1764. Honoured by the Convention with the title of French citizen for his enthusiastic championship of revolutionary principles in Corsica, he seems to have joined the Society of the Panthéon in 1795.   Sylvain Maréchal was the orator and professional demagogue of the party.   Even before 1789 he had served four months' imprisonment for the publication of his *Almanach des honnêtes gens*, and had written an " Atheist's Dictionary ".   He became one of the leading orators of the Panthéon, and his permanent importance for the story of Babouvism is that he wrote its popular songs and drafted the famous *Manifeste des Égaux*, the prelude to the plot.   Debon is a shadowy figure in the whole story, but Félix Le Pelletier, who did so much to finance the movement, was brother of the more famous Louis Michel Le Pelletier de Saint Fargeau, member of the Convention, who was assassinated in a café the day after the execution of Louis XVI in 1793.   Félix escaped both imprisonment and execution, and stood by Babeuf's family financially after the execution of Babeuf.

These then were the conspirators : a strange medley of hardened plotters and experienced revolutionaries, none of them with much to lose by insurrection, apart from Le Pelletier, and all of them sincere in their egalitarian ideals. In this company, the acknowledged ideological head of the new " Secret Directory " as the committee was called, " Gracchus " Babeuf reached the apex of his career. He had emerged from the mass of discontented and frustrated demagogues and journalists, and had taken his place as the centre of an active new movement, with a band of disciples ready to follow him—as some of them did—to the death. His natural capacity for leadership had asserted itself.

The rank-and-file sympathizers of the Babouvists—the subscribers to the *Tribun* and the outer ring of the movement—were predominantly middle class and artisan, with a sprinkling of workers and idlers and mere ruffians. Personal grievances and personal motives of hatred of the Directory and the *nouveaux riches* seem to have been more often the reasons for their support than positive agreement with Babeuf's communistic principles and theories. Professor A. Mathiez has analysed the list of 642 subscribers to Babeuf's journal—a list six times bigger than that of subscribers to the conservative pro-government organ, *L'Orateur constitutionnel*.[1] He discovered that both lists were drawn from precisely the same social classes— business men, manufacturers, *fonctionnaires* of all grades, small tradesmen and professional men such as lawyers and doctors. The *Tribun* list includes many of the old *Montagnards*, the Robespierrists, and the professional army. They were drawn from all over the country except the

[1] Cf. *Revue des Cours et Conférences, 1928–1929*, p. 559 ff.

west, and most thickly from areas where the White Terror had been strongest. What the Babeuf Plot mobilized in its support was not the people who wanted a communist order in France, for these were but few : it was a whole section of the discontented middle and artisan class, seeking revenge against the reactionary forces of Thermidor. Prominent in the list are widows of guillotined revolutionaries and former agents of the Terror who had been imprisoned by the Directory. Their main interest was personal vengeance against the Government. The letters Babeuf received from many of his supporters confirm this verdict : they expressed disagreement or mere bewilderment with all the talk of Equality, but they thoroughly approved his invective against the Directory.

The favourite rendezvous of the conspirators and their associates was the Café des Bains-Chinois. Charles Germain later gave a vivid description of the place to which justice can be done only in the original French.

Il existe sur le boulevard du théâtre italien, au coin de la rue de la Michaudière, en face de celle du Mont-Blanc, un bâtiment de structure orientale. C'est là qu'était autrefois l'établissment des bains chinois. La façade de cet édifice pique et attache la curiosité de tous les passants. Chacun s'y arrête pour bâiller aux colifichets qui s'offrent tout-à-coup à sa vue. Des magots de la Chine, au front largement chauve, à la poitrine ombragée d'une barbe épaisse, des parasols adroitement découpés, une innombrable multitude de clochettes, d'inintelligibles hiéroglyphes, des pavillons artistement peints, des balcons, des treillages, des sols artificiels, en voilà bien autant qu'il en faut pour forcer la multitude des badauds à stationner devant cette burlesque habitation. Le café se trouve au rez de chaussée, et par le nombre de ses vitraux, ressemble assez à une cage ouverte à tous les regards. Devant, derrière, sur les flancs, sont de grandes portes de glaces transparentes. À sept ou huit pas de la principale porte d'entrée, et sur la façade du boulevard, d'élégantes marchandes de mode ont fixé leur temple de toilettes, dans lequel la foule des amateurs et amatrices se presse à toutes les heures du jour et de la nuit. À quelques pas de là est un nombreux corps-de-garde. À trois portées de fusil, sur la gauche, rue Neuve-des-Capucines, se trouvaient alors, en germinal, l'état-major général de l'armée parisienne, les bureaux des commissaires de guerre, le département de la Seine, et le ministre de la justice, un des hôtels de la trésorerie nationale, établissements qui provoquaient dans le quartier une plus grande et plus active surveillance, un concours non interrompu de patrouilles à pied et à cheval, de vedettes, de factionnaires et d'espions de la police. À droite, à deux portées de fusil au-dessus du café, est la fameuse promenade qui, par la fréquentation habituelle de tous les agioteurs, de tous les escrocs, de toutes les luxueuses prostituées, a mérité le sobriquet de *Petit-Coblentz*. Je conviens qu'il est difficile de douter qu'un site plus avantageux puisse ailleurs se rencontrer pour conspirer en une sécurité parfaite.

Here many of the more popular Babouvist songs were launched upon Paris. Here one of the singers at the Chinese-Baths café, pretty, red-haired Sophie Lapierre, who was alleged to be Darthé's mistress, would sing political verses composed for her by Darthé or Maréchal.

> Tu nous créas pour être égaux,
> Nature, ô bienfaisante mère !
> Pourquoi des biens et des travaux
> L'inégalité meurtrière ?

Pourquoi mille esclaves rampants
Autour de quatre à cinq despotes ?
Pourquoi des petits et des grands ?
Levez-vous braves sans-culottes.

This was the grotesque atmosphere in which the Babeuf
Plot was hatched.

The story of the plot begins in April 1796, with the
preparation of the *Manifeste des Égaux*, drawn up by
Sylvain Maréchal. Not every detail of the Manifesto was
approved by the whole committee ; but there is no
evidence that Babeuf disapproved of any part of it, and it
became the most famous—if not the most coherent—of all
expressions of Babouvist doctrine. It merits comparison
with that far more important manifesto of communism
which Marx and Engels were to publish over fifty years
later. But the " Manifesto of the Equals " best speaks for
itself. With some repetitions and rhetoric omitted (the
full French text can be read in the works of either
Advielle or Buonarroti mentioned on page 107), it runs
as follows :

People of France !
For fifteen centuries you have lived as slaves and
therefore in misery. For six years you have stood
breathless, waiting for independence, happiness and
equality.
EQUALITY ! ! the first desire of nature, the first
need of man, chief bond of all legitimate society !
People of France ! you have not been favoured above
other nations which vegetate in this unhappy world !
. . . From time immemorial we have been told—
hypocritically—that men are equal ; and from time
immemorial inequality of the most degrading and
most monstrous kind has insolently weighed on man-

kind. Ever since there have been civil societies man's finest birthright has been recognized without contradiction but so far has not once been carried into effect : equality was nothing more than a legal fiction, beautiful but sterile. To-day when our clamour for it is more resolute, we are told " Hold your tongues, wretches ! real equality is only an illusion ; content yourselves with conditional equality : you are all equal before the law. *Canaille !* what more do you need ? " Well ! what more do we need ? Now listen in your turn, legislators, rulers and rich proprietors. . . .

We claim in future to live and die, as we are born, equals : we want true equality or death ; that is what we must have. And we will have equality whatever the price. Woe to those who stand between it and us ! Woe to whoever would resist a wish so pronounced !

The French Revolution is only the forerunner of another revolution far greater, far more solemn, which will be the last.

The people have trampled on the bodies of kings and priests allied against them : it will be the same for the new tyrants, the new political hypocrites sitting in the places of the old.

What is it that we need in addition to equality of rights ?

We need not only that equality be written out in the Declaration of the Rights of Man and of the Citizen, we want it in our very midst, in our hearths and homes. We will pay any price for it, to make a clean sweep so that we can cherish it alone. If need be let all the arts perish so long as true equality remains ! . . .

The agrarian law or the distribution of lands was

the unconsidered wish of a few unprincipled soldiers, of a few small groups prompted by instinct rather than by reason. We aspire to something more sublime and more just, THE COMMON GOOD OR THE COMMUNITY OF GOODS ! No more individual owner-ship of land, the land belongs to nobody. We lay claim to, we demand, common enjoyment of the fruits of the earth : these fruits exist for all.

We declare that we can no longer suffer the great majority of men to toil and sweat in the service of the few and for the pleasure of the small minority. . . . Begone, henceforth, monstrous distinctions of rich and poor, of great and small, of masters and servants, of rulers and ruled.

Let there be no differences between human beings other than age and sex. Since all have the same needs and the same faculties, let there be one educa-tion, one fare for all. They are satisfied with one sun, one air, why should not the same quantity and quality of food suffice for each ? . . .

People of France !

No more vast design has ever been conceived and carried out. On rare occasions a few men of genius, a few wise men, have spoken of it in whispers, trembling. Not one had the courage to tell the whole truth.

The time for greatness has come. The evil is at its height ; it covers the face of the earth. . . . The moment has come to found the REPUBLIC OF EQUALS, that great hospice open to all men. The days of general restitution have come. Come all ye in distress and be seated at the common table set by nature for all her children.

People of France !

The highest of all glories is yours ! Yes, it is you

who must be the first to offer the world this moving
sight. . . .

On the morrow of this true revolution, men will
say to each other in amazement : What ! was the
common good to be had for so little ? We had only
to will it. Ah ! why did we not will it sooner ? Why
had we to be told so many times ? Without doubt
while there is still a single man in the whole world
who is richer and more powerful than his fellows or
equals, he destroys this equilibrium : crime and
misery remain upon the earth.

People of France !

By what sign then will you henceforth recognize
the excellence of a constitution ? Only one that
rests entirely on real equality will be good enough
for you and will satisfy all your desires. The aristocratic charters of 1791 and 1795 rivet your chains
instead of breaking them. That of 1793 made a real
stride towards true equality ; never before had it
been so closely approached ; but it still had not
attained the goal, and did not begin to realize the
common good, although it was solemnly consecrated
to that great principle.

People of France !

Open your eyes and hearts to full felicity : recognize and proclaim with us the REPUBLIC OF EQUALS.

Here was an open challenge to the whole established
order, and to all that the Revolution had achieved so far.
In the circumstances of 1796 it was a clarion call to action
—to rescue all that was most appealing to the social ideals
of the Revolution while there was yet time. Its keynotes
are that equality is essential for the achievement of liberty,
and that it *can* be achieved—as the natural order of things
—merely by resolute action immediately. It breathed of

revolution as no pronouncement had done since those far-off days when the National Assembly had drawn up the Declaration of the Rights of Man.

The committee, probably guided by Babeuf, followed this Manifesto of Maréchal with a more officially endorsed, much less rhetorical and more incisive statement of the doctrines of Babouvism. Babeuf later denied that he was its author, but accepted its terms. The *Analyse de la doctrine de Babeuf*, stated simply under a dozen heads, runs as follows:

1. Nature has given every man an equal right to the enjoyment of all wealth.
2. The aim of society is to defend this equality, often attacked by the strong and the wicked in the state of nature, and to increase, by the co-operation of all, this enjoyment.
3. Nature has imposed on each man the duty to work ; no one can, without committing a crime, abstain from working.
4. Labour and enjoyment ought to be in common.
5. Oppression exists when one man exhausts himself working and wants for everything, while another wallows in abundance without doing anything.
6. No one can, without committing a crime, appropriate to himself alone the wealth of the earth or of industry.
7. In a true society there should be neither rich nor poor.
8. The rich who will not give up their superfluity to help the needy are enemies of the people.
9. No one should be able, by monopolizing the means, to deprive another of the education necessary for his happiness ; education ought to be in common.
10. The aim of the Revolution is to destroy inequality and establish the common happiness.
11. The Revolution is not finished, because the rich absorb

C

all wealth and rule exclusively, while the poor work like veritable slaves, languishing in poverty and counting for nothing in the State.

12. The constitution of 1793 is the true law of the French nation, because the People have solemnly accepted it.

These two documents, taken together, became the authentic texts of Babouvism. It is noteworthy that neither, so far as is known, was actually written by Babeuf himself, though he apparently endorsed all their sentiments. But in the exact nuances of these statements lay the seeds of later divergences of interpretation and textual criticism which were to make Babouvism something other than the personal beliefs of Babeuf. Just as Karl Marx was later to declare " I am not a Marxist ", so might Babeuf have come to deny, in time, that he was a Babouvist.

So far—words : fine, rhetorical words, occasionally incisive and telling words, but only words. What of deeds ? The actual conspiracy, to which these declarations were only the prelude, bore no immediate fruit. It was exploded before it occurred. But what the conspirators achieved in the short time of one month is very remarkable ; and the method of insurrection that they devised and practised in this short time was a landmark in revolutionary technique.

The two essential principles of action were the concentration of power and planning in the hands of a small central committee, and the use of picked revolutionary agents to penetrate, propagand and win over the army, police, and other branches of the machinery of State. It was to be a truly modern *coup d'état*. It was carefully prepared by intensive propaganda. By placards and flysheets the *Analyse* and its doctrines were widely disseminated. Tracts asked, and answered in the negative, such questions as *Do we owe obedience to the Constitution of the Year III ?* The snowstorm of Babouvist publications was welcomed by thousands in distress and ready for upheaval. They were seized on and read eagerly in workshops and barracks. Propaganda concentrated particularly on the army, and here it is plain that Babeuf and Buonarroti were too academic and abstract to cut much ice. Their tracts went above the heads of the soldiers ; even when they were delivered personally by the prostitutes of Grenelle. The shrewdest advice and the cleverest propaganda for this purpose came from one Grisel. Concentrate, he advised, on that third of the army which was composed of professional fighters, caring nothing for whom they fought or under what régime so long as they could secure plenty of pillage. Talk to them, he urged, not of liberty and equality, but of poor pay, tyrannical orders, poverty when they return home. The coarse, homely, penetrating propaganda devised by Georges Grisel, himself an army captain, reveals him as a worthy predecessor to Dr. Goebbels. He alone had grasped the fact that propaganda of this inflammatory kind must appeal to the crudest mass-emotions and the most material of motives ; and he alone, before Bonaparte, saw how utterly dependent on military backing any *coup* must be.

The vital link in the plan was the band of twelve revolutionary agents. Their task was to supervise propaganda in each *arrondissement*, to report regularly—even daily— on the state of public opinion, to form cells of insurgents in the military " legion of police " stationed in Paris, in the barracks at Grenelle just outside the city, and in private houses. The agents chosen were no more " proletarian " in origin or character than the central conspirators themselves. They were nearly all men of the lesser bourgeoisie and artisan class—former *fonctionnaires*, police, soldiers, professional men, and small tradesmen such as tailors and printers. They varied greatly in efficiency and reliability. Babeuf's chief lieutenants in the work were Darthé and Charles Germain, his friends since his days in Arras prison. In these last-minute efforts to whip up widespread backing for the revolt violence and pillage came to be emphasized more than before in Babouvist propaganda ; and it is on the writings and appeals of this period that the opponents of Babeuf can most happily base their charges of reckless incitement to bloodshed.

In April, two battalions of the " legion of police " were, contrary to the law, removed from Paris by the Government because Babouvist ideas had spread disaffection in their ranks. This aroused so much agitation that the battalions had to be dissolved. Fear of being sent to the fighting fronts was a fear on which Babouvist propaganda could effectively play. From this valuable material the conspirators were able to recruit an advance guard of trained fighters. So tense was the atmosphere of revolt that public meetings and demonstrations began to be held in defiance of the Government. Paris seemed ripe for yet another revolution ; and it was still only the end of April.

On May 1, special military advisers were summoned together by the conspirators to plan the *coup de grâce*. Germain and Grisel were the chief, but they included also Rossignol, Massart and Fion. They met together with Babeuf, Buonarroti, Darthé, Maréchal, Debon and Didier. A special military committee of the five " technicians " was appointed. Germain remained the special intermediary between this committee and the Secret Directory. Yet a third committee had been set up independently among the former members of the " Mountain," the old Jacobins, and efforts were made to reach agreement between Jacobins and Babouvists. Darthé and Ricord served as intermediaries here. Agreement was not reached between them until May 7. The following day—

May 8—a general meeting of the three insurrectionary committees, Jacobin, Babouvist and military, was held. It lasted from eight until a quarter to eleven in the evening, and agreed on final plans for the rising. It was planned to meet again two days later and fix an exact time for the *coup*. It was estimated that a force of 17,000 men could be relied upon absolutely, and that the masses of the lower middle class and working class all over Paris would rally to this revolutionary force once it began to move.

The preparations were remarkably thorough. A store of arms and ammunition had been laid up, and plans were all ready for the speedy seizure of Government dumps of weapons. Members of the Jacobin party had been summoned from all over the country to Paris, ready to serve as reinforcements for the popular insurrection. Lyons was a particularly hopeful source of recruitment, and its former Jacobin Mayor, Bertrand, served as recruiting agent. An *Acte insurrecteur*, or programme of revolt, had been laboriously drafted by the Secret Directory, ready for issue to the people at the moment of revolt. It was enormously long-winded and verbose, but the gist of the plan was the sudden violent overthrow of the existing government by the seizure of its leading members, and the installation of the " Insurrectionary Committee of Public Safety ", composed of the " Secret Directory ", in its stead. Its object was defined as the re-establishment of " the Constitution of 1793, the liberty, equality and happiness of all ". To the summons of tocsin and trumpet, and behind banners bearing this slogan, citizens from each district of Paris were to march with their arms or any available weapons to the chief places of the *arrondissements*. The national treasury, the post, the houses of ministers and every public building were to be seized. Bakers were to be requisitioned to bake bread, which would be distributed free to the people. Any attempt of the old authorities to continue to exercise power was declared illegal, and was to be punished by death. All resistance was to be ruthlessly crushed. This achieved, the Insurrectionary Committee would remain in power until a new National Assembly could be elected. And it was to be announced that " the task of ending the Revolution and giving the Republic Liberty, Equality, and the Constitution of 1793, shall be confided to a National Assembly, composed of one democrat for each *département*, elected by the insurrectionary people on the nomination of the Insurrectionary Committee."

But from May 1, when the military experts were appointed as a special committee, until May 10, the day chosen for the second and final joint meeting of the three insurrectionary committees, the Government was kept very fully informed of the plans of the conspirators, and was only waiting for the right moment to strike. The chief informer was Grisel, skilful propagandist and leading member of the military committee. He was not the only squealer : the proprietor of the that Café des Bains-Chinois favourite rendezvous of the Babouvists, was also a regular informer, and there were all the usual police spies who eavesdropped on café conversations. Even with these enormous advantages—which were by no means one-sided, for the Babouvists in turn had their spies in the police organizations and elsewhere—the Directory and the Ministry of Police very nearly bungled the exposure of the plot. The first joint meeting on May 8 had just dispersed before Cochon, the Minister of Police, with a troop of soldiers, broke into the house to find only Darthé and Drouet, the occupier of the house. The raid was called off, as neither Darthé nor Drouet was worth arresting on his own. Thoroughly alarmed, the conspirators had been reassured by Grisel that both previous governmental inactivity and this blunder were reasons for confidence that no serious knowledge of the plot had come to the ears of the police. In any case it was now too late to draw back and there seemed every reason for hastening on the preparations. Accordingly, when the final joint meeting was duly held on the 10th a body of soldiers invaded the house and arrested all the leading conspirators except Babeuf and Buonarotti, who were not present. They had taken refuge at the house of the tailor Tissot, at 21 Rue de la Grande Truanderie ; but there they too were found and arrested by the police.

On the same day, May 10, Carnot, the most powerful man in the Government, sent a message to the Council of the Five Hundred announcing that a dastardly plot had been hatched to overthrow the Constitution, massacre the legislative body, the Government and the military leaders of the State, and deliver up Paris to mob rule. Immediately after the arrests the Press gave lurid accounts of the plot and its purpose. Two days after his arrest, having assumed full responsibility for the plot in order to shield his associates, Babeuf wrote to the Directory a letter which for impudence must be unique in the annals of insurrection. He claimed, in short, that his power was as great as theirs, and appealed for joint action by the Government and the conspirators to establish true democracy in France. The important passages are worth quotation. He began :

Citizens and Directors : Would you regard it as beneath you to treat with me as between power and power ? You have now seen the mighty confidence which is placed in me ! You have seen that my party may well equal yours. . . . What would happen if this affair should be revealed in full daylight ? I would assume the most glorious of all roles ! I would demonstrate, with all my power and all the energy that you know me to have, the righteousness of the conspiracy of which I have never denied being the ringleader. Leaving that cowardly course strewn with denials, which the common run of accused utilize as self-justification, I would dare to develop great principles, plead the eternal rights of the people. . . . Whatever my fate, my name will rank beside those of Barnevelt and Sidney ; and whether I am led to death or exile, I am certain of immortality. . . . I see but one policy that is wise for you to follow. Declare that there has never been any serious conspiracy. Five men, thus showing themselves great and generous, can to-day save the country. . . . You know how much influence I have with this class of men—with the patriots. Well, I will use it to convince them that if you are at one with the people, they ought to act at one with you. Surely it will be no unhappy solution if this simple letter were to pacify the internal situation in France, by checking the notoriety of this affair. Would it not, at the same time, stop all that is now opposed to the pacification of Europe ?

Whatever may be said against this effusion—whether it be interpreted as a last-minute gamble to try to save his ideals or merely himself—two things are certain. Babeuf lacked neither courage nor imagination ; and it was completely in vain. It may, indeed, be explained partly by the knowledge that Barras, one of the five Directors, had himself been well in with the later stage of the conspiracy, and so might yet act as a link between plotters and Government. But Barras was too busily engaged concocting a speedy alibi, and was only too anxious to whitewash himself by rebutting any suggestion of a compromise. The other four—especially Carnot—were resolved to crush the whole conspiracy with utter ruthlessness.

Drouet, in whose house the conspirators had been meeting, was a member of the Council of the Five Hundred—the legislative body—as well as a former member of the " Mountain " in the Convention. For his trial, a special high court had to be set up according to the Constitution. The Government decided that all conspirators should therefore be tried before such a special tribunal held at Vendôme ; though Drouet meanwhile escaped from prison, no doubt with the connivance of Barras, who was anxious to prevent the public trial of a man who might implicate himself. There were two or three hundred arrests ; and with all the organizers of the plot lodged in gaol, all hope of the insurrection happening " spontaneously " faded away.

There were only two further resorts to violence, both doomed to failure. On May 26 the members on the fringe of the conspiracy who were still at large tried to stage a rescue of the Babouvists, without avail. Again, on September 7, some hundreds of Babeuf's followers planned to seize the palace of the Luxembourg, official residence of the Directory, and then call on the disaffected soldiers at Grenelle to rally to their support. But again the initial attack failed due to efficient police espionage. A volley of fire from the camp at Grenelle dispersed the mob and killed over a hundred of its members. The last flicker of armed insurrection died out, and the great Revolution came at last to an end.

Could the Babeuf plot have succeeded ? Given the unsuspected presence of a spy like Grisel in its midst, it was of course virtually doomed. But apart from this factor, was it foredoomed to failure from the start ? The question remains open. One of its weaknesses was lack of finance. To succeed by force it was not enough to win

c*

over the bulk of the organized army : it had to secure support by paying the soldiers. This the plotters hoped to do by seizing the national treasury and requisitioning food supplies. But before that was possible, shortage of money was a handicap.

A more mortal weakness was internal dissension—especially between Babouvist egalitarians and the old Jacobins. The two forces which drew together for the climax of the plot were different in both temper and ideology, and many of the Jacobins still favoured caution. The Babouvists were very optimistic. They tended to exaggerate the amount of working-class support they would get because their movement centred in the faubourg Saint-Antoine, which was an exceptional industrial area. They over-estimated the amount of provincial support they would get, because of the large number of subscribers to the *Tribun* ; but the motives for buying the *Tribun*, as already shown, were not normally communistic motives. They overrated, too, the extent of sympathy in the army ; there, too, discontent was very general, but it did not necessarily involve desire for the " Republic of Equals " as visualized by Babeuf. He thought of a social revolution as no more difficult to achieve than a political *coup*, and despite his own earlier analysis he overlooked the forces both of inertia and of positive hostility which such a social revolution would encounter. The more experienced Jacobins, recalling the difficulties of Robespierre and anxious to evade the guillotine, were less confident.

On the other hand, the conspirators had great elements of strength. If they were divided so too was the Government—as witness the early preparations of the flashy and amorous Director, Barras, for well-timed defection. The supporters of the Directory were divided between the *nouveaux riches*, the main beneficiaries of the secularization

BARRAS.

Face p. 42

of Church lands and the sequestration of nobles' property ; and the conservative, royalist forces who preferred the rule of the Directory to further excesses and the threat of disorder, but who would have preferred a constitutional monarchy to either. The Directory tried to rally the moderate conservatives of all parties to support of the Government by magnifying and dwelling upon the anarchy which would follow its downfall. Royalists and Babouvists alike became bogies of disorder, and the Directory astutely mobilized all beneficiaries of the Revolution in defence of its own power. The Royalists were, of course, quite distinct in personnel, aims and organization from the disciples of Babeuf ; but from the point of view of the peasantry and the wealthy bourgeoisie both were equally detestable and scarifying. Both were out of tune with the trend of events in 1796 ; which was towards the military dictatorship of General Bonaparte. Indeed the scare of the Babeuf Plot, skilfully exploited by the Government and the Government Press, did something to drive France into the arms of Napoleon.

In judging the over-optimism and clumsiness of the conspirators, it is important to recall that they were not only for the most part intellectuals and doctrinaire agitators, but men who had been in prison a lot and so tended to be out of touch with public opinion, and with the realities of politics in 1796.

Before considering the trial of the conspirators, which launched the legend of Babouvism as a permanent political force, it is necessary to say something of the political ideas of the Babouvists as presented in their own writings. As already suggested, the actual political creed and proposals of Babeuf and his personal disciples are distinct from the later elaboration of Babouvism. The former may be briefly summarized as follows.

In his earlier more technical writings, such as the *Cadastre perpétuel* and the *Correspondant Picard*, elements of certain communistic beliefs and theories can be discerned. It has been suggested that these were no more than Babeuf had learnt from the strong communal life of the Picardy peasants. But it is likely that Babeuf's mind, under the pressure of personal frustration and bitter experience, was gradually tending more and more towards virtual communism during the years prior to 1795. Too much, indeed, has been made of these early signs by certain writers ; but they are significant enough. Thus, in 1787 he wrote to Dubois de Fosseux advocating abolition of the right of inheritance.

> Each [citizen] on death would make the whole of Society the heir of all his property, and no one would any longer want to see his next of kin die in order that he might have the double advantage of enjoying what they would have possessed, and of putting other aspirants in the position of acquiring the same desires.

Four years later he wrote in the *Correspondant Picard* :

> The constitution must be a national patrimony, where there is bread both of the spirit and of the body for the people as a whole, where a guarantee of complete intellectual and material life is not only made clear, precise and positive, but also is immediately sanctioned by the placing in common of all resources which have indefinably multiplied and accumulated through an organization intelligently contrived and general labour wisely directed.

The interest of these early essays into communistic ideas is that they were the consequence of pressing one stage further the characteristically philanthropic theories of the eighteenth-century *philosophes*. The starting-point of all

Babeuf's arguments is that men are born free and equal, that the *ancien régime* with its elaborate system of classes and privileges has frustrated this natural order of things, and that once men are made free and equal, under a democratic constitution, the general happiness will result. What is distinctive about Babeuf is his insistence, from an early stage of his writings even before the outbreak of the Revolution, that attention must be paid not merely to political forms and new republican constitutions, but also to the problems of economics : to the organization of production and labour, to land tenure, and to the distribution of wealth within the community. The typical eighteenth-century creed was that political reforms must come first, and that then social and economic distress and inequality would remedy themselves. Babeuf was always somewhat sceptical of this priority of revolutionary purpose. But until the experience of the Terror, and still more of the Directory, he did not place this scepticism in the forefront of his beliefs. He continued to speak in the typical vocabulary of the enlightenment until the events of 1794 and 1795 edged him ever nearer to complete communism. Even then, until the end of 1795, he got little further than insisting that political and social questions are inseparable ; which was a considerable advance on normal eighteenth-century political thought in France. He did not leap forward to the economic determinism of Marxist communism.

In his political creed he always remained essentially a Jacobin. He believed that sovereignty should in practice lie where " by the law of nature " it does lie—in the general will of the whole community. This was emphasized by his return to faith in the fundamental virtue of Robespierre, after his temporary disillusionment with the Reign of Terror. He believed in the natural goodness of man, hampered and frustrated only by the evils of environment, by bad economic and political institutions which allowed the vices of greed and tyranny to prevail. He was utopian in that he not only looked forward to a golden age, but also believed that the golden age was round the corner and was France's just for the asking and the making. The dynamism of his appeals lay—like that of Marxism later—in his presenting communism as an immediately practicable and attainable system.

In Number 35 of the *Tribun du Peuple* (published on November 30, 1795) Babeuf first embarked consistently on out-and-out communist theories. Insisting that *l'égalité de fait n'est pas un chimère* and that when Jean-Jacques wrote *Pour que l'état social soit perfectionné, il faut que chacun ait assez, et qu'aucun n'ait trop* he was pointing to the very essence of the social contract, he proceeded to outline a very naïve communism. There must be no privation in those goods which Nature has given for the enjoyment of all : and where, by the inevitable accidents of nature, there is a natural shortage, then the consequent hardship must be borne equally by all. The only road to justice and equality is to establish an *administration commune* : to suppress private property ; to allocate to each man the work for which he is best fitted, for all work essential to the community is equally honourable ; and to oblige him to deposit the produce of his labours in a common pool. Then all that is needed is a simple agency for distribution of supplies which, " keeping a register of all individuals and of all goods, will partition these goods according to the strictest principles of equality and deliver them to the home of each individual". Under such a government boundaries and locked doors, crime and punishment, law-suits and prisons, envy and hatred, will all disappear. The golden age will begin.

On these airy visions of an ideal communism, which were elaborated in the next few issues of the *Tribun* along

with increasingly virulent attacks on the existing government and the old order of things, a " practical programme " for achieving such communism came to be
built. It must begin, clearly, with seizure of power by
those who have seen this vision most clearly. The existing
government would be overthrown and all forces of resistance crushed. There is no doubt that Babeuf—possibly
carried away by his own exuberant writings—gravely
overestimated the ease with which such an upheaval
could be effected. Men like Darthé and Buonarroti
pointed out the practical difficulties which Robespierre
had met with in his attempt to enforce the Laws of the
Maximum. Evasions, sabotage and a serious drop in
production would be the result—especially among the
peasants who produced the food. But Babeuf seems to
have been undaunted in his optimism.

The concrete programme was expressed very clearly in
the two draft decrees which were to be issued as soon as
the insurrection had succeeded. First, a " great national
community of wealth " was to be established in the
Republic. It would include all existing public buildings
and national property ; hospitals and schools ; all
voluntary surrenders of private property ; all property
sequestered from those who had been enriching themselves in the public services ; all lands left uncultivated
by their owners. All citizens would be invited to surrender their wealth voluntarily to the community, and
could become full citizens only after they had done so.
The poor and destitute would automatically be citizens,
as would all people over sixty years of age.

Inheritance was to be immediately abolished, and all
private property would revert to the community on the
death of its existing owners. Private property would thus
gradually wither away in one generation ; and meanwhile
property-owners who did not surrender their property

were to be debarred from full citizenship, and disqualified from civil or military office. The national community would at once guarantee to all its full members an equal and adequate livelihood. In return, every member of the community would have to pledge himself to perform all labour of which he was capable in agriculture or industry. There would be occupational grouping of all citizens and each group would elect its own officials to organize and regulate the conditions of production, and supervise the equal distribution of all wealth produced. Territorially there were to be communal local authorities, responsible for local administration and for executing the laws of the central authority. They would organize communal meals and supervise the occupational groups within the area. Above these there would be regional groupings of the *départements*, determined on economic lines, to co-ordinate production and distribution in the *départements*, and to act as liaison with the central authority. All foreign trade would be in the hands of the national authority alone. Persons not members of the community would alone be liable to taxation, and this taxation would double each year until they were taxed down to the general level of the community. The national debt would be wiped out for all Frenchmen, but foreign creditors would be paid off. No more money would be coined, and neither gold nor silver would in future be imported into France.

In a sense even this naïve and drastic revolutionary programme was conceivable and practicable enough in the fluid, desperate conditions of France in 1796. Given the crash of the *assignats*, the seething popular revolutionary forces, and the fanaticism of the Babouvists, it is a programme which would certainly have been attempted had power been effectively grasped on May 11, 1796. It would have met with last-ditch resistance from all the wealthy classes, old and new. The peasants who had satisfied so much of their land-hunger, the bourgeoisie who had profited from the division of lands, would have been violently opposed to this communistic reversal of the distributions already carried out. It could not have been seriously attempted without extensive bloodshed—a fact which the Babouvists recognized in their more realistic moods. Given the prolongation of the foreign war, it is improbable that France, any more than the Russia of Kerensky and Luov in 1917, could have long maintained both war and revolution at the same time. In this respect the programme of the Babouvists was doubtless doomed to failure from the start. The Powers of Europe would have sustained a war of intervention until the experiment was killed, had it ever been even launched.

Although in basis philanthropic and universalist, like all eighteenth-century thought, Babouvism was not in practice international. It was not for export in any foreseeable future, and made no appeal for " workers of the world to unite ". It was nationalist in temper and purpose, and visualized no revolutionary action beyond the frontier other than the mere force of example. Only in the hands of Buonarroti a generation later did Babouvism acquire an international appeal.

The Babouvism of Babeuf owed none of its importance to originality of ideas or to systematization of thought. Egalitarian and even communistic ideas were very much in the air in the 1790's. Many men, whose names are now generally forgotten, were putting forward proposals for communization of land and industry, for seeking the reign of perfect equality. These have been admirably described by Dr. André Lichtenberger fifty years ago, but the names of the men who made them are still lost in oblivion.[1] A more prominent contemporary of Babeuf,

[1] Cf. André Lichtenberger : *Le Socialisme au XVIIIe Siècle* (1895), *Le Socialisme Utopique* (1898), and *Le Socialisme et la Révolution Française* (1899).

Simon-Nicolas-Henri Linguet, evolved a much more systematic and penetrating analysis of society than Babeuf, but it had little or no effect on history. A lawyer who, like Babeuf, became a popular journalist and who eventually, also like Babeuf, ended his life on the scaffold, Linguet had begun his attacks on law and property as early as 1763. From 1777 until 1784 he published his *Annales* which combined sustained invective against the existing order with communistic propaganda. But although he spoke in terms of the class war, of the need to abolish private property before justice could be achieved in society, the conclusion he drew was that even a communist revolution would be so unlikely to produce human happiness that things were better left as they were after all ! Between the extremes of utopian optimism and such bleak pessimism, there was but one creed which contemplated immediate concrete action : and that was Babouvism. This is its main importance.

As the Babouvist programme shows, Babeuf retained even in economic matters the eighteenth-century faith in the power of organizational devices and reforms to effect the transformation of society. He had no developed theory of a class war, as had Linguet ; no doctrine of any inherent cleavage between the owners of the means of production and those who had only their labour to sell. He did not visualize the labouring classes as a " proletariat ", though it was his nineteenth-century disciple, Auguste Blanqui, who was to coin the phrase " dictatorship of the proletariat ". His analysis was the simpler one of the gulf between rich and poor—a distinction which would automatically disappear once the right machinery had been contrived for systematic equalization of wealth. The devices he proposed—the abolition of inheritance, the imposition of very steeply graded taxation, and social regulation of labour conditions, hours of work and rewards—are little more than extreme applications of the principles which the modern social-service State, of whatever political structure, has come increasingly to adopt. It is of this development—the evolution of the positive social-service State, guaranteeing to all its citizens a basic subsistence level and providing social services for all "according to needs"—that Babeuf and his colleagues were the real prophets. He was not, in basic theory, the apostle of Marxist communism. His golden age was to be inaugurated by one incisive *coup de main*, but thereafter was to develop by voluntary surrender of property rights. Even the original revolution was to be achieved largely by the spontaneous insurrection of the popular masses. It is in choice of method rather than of aim—in elaboration of the technique of revolution—that the Babouvists were historically the precursors of modern Marxists. The attention to preparation by propaganda, the use of methods of infiltration and permeation through local cells of activist supporters, the direction of operations by a small central committee, are in combination the most important Babouvist contribution to the technique of revolution. This was to become the patient and perpetual study of the large class of professional revolutionaries in nineteenth-century Europe.[1] From them and through them, the technique was passed on to the modern Communists, by whom it was perfected and used to such striking effect in 1917. The Babouvists were amateurs in

[1] Subsequent experimentation in the new technique of revolution during the nineteenth century can be studied in such works as E. H. Carr : *The Romantic Exiles* (1933) and *Michael Bakunin* (1937) ; David Footman : *Red Prelude* (1944) ; and of course the whole story of Lenin's career and of the Bolshevik Revolution in Russia. The development of it by Babouvist disciples such as Buonarroti and Blanqui is briefly dealt with below. It must be remembered, however, that revolutionary procedure and strategy evolved step by step with the evolution of the modern State, whatever the form of its régime ; and it probably owed less to precedent and example than fervent students of the subject care to admit, and much more to *ad hoc* adaptation to the mode of government which revolutionaries have to defeat.

the matter of timing, of adequate security measures, and of patient, painstaking preparation for the revolutionary moment. But they gave both the example and the warning. Never again could revolutions be anything but a matter for the trained expert, if they were to have any hope of success.

The course of French history in the nineteenth century gave one stratum after another in French society an interest in the technique of secret organization and underground resistance. In the decade between 1820 and 1830, when France was ruled by the restored Bourbons, it was the respectable bourgeois Liberals who were driven into subterranean opposition. Men like the great Lafayette and the aristocratic d'Argenson associated themselves with military plots and demonstrations against the rule of the *émigrés*. Under the July Monarchy of Louis Philippe after 1830, it was the more radical Republicans who formed secret societies, and joined with the new forces of socialism against the conservative rule of Guizot. After 1848, it was left to the organized socialist and communist movements to agitate for more sweeping reforms ; and under the Second Empire, Liberals, Radicals and Socialists mingled in a joint opposition to the dictatorship of Napoleon III. Each new régime of nineteenth-century France left large and increasingly important classes dissatisfied, and the repression of agitation among these classes gave birth to underground resistance. In this way each stratum—and ultimately each major political party —was encouraged to look to past experience of republican conspiracy. That is why the legend of Babeuf was perpetuated—why the *mystique* of Babouvism grew—and why, as will be seen, most republican parties of modern France have claimed Babeuf as in some measure their own.

Chapter III

THE LAUNCHING OF A LEGEND

IF the events of 1796 revealed the nature, formation and *débâcle* of the Babouvist conspiracy, the events of 1797 ensured that the ideas and personalities of the conspirators should not be forgotten. Indeed the warning that Babeuf had given the Directory in his letter written two days after his arrest came to be justified. He became " certain of immortality ". The course of the trial of the Babouvists, and the behaviour of the leaders at their execution, appended to the whole story a highly explosive emotional charge which gave impetus to the legend of Babouvism. The story of the great political trial, which has topical interest in view of the political trials in modern Europe, is in tune with the experience of all such trials. Political trials are always difficult to keep under control ; and the longer they last, the more difficult is control over their effects.

The trial began on February 20, 1797, and lasted until May 27 of the same year.[1] The prisoners had been kept in the Vendôme prison from August 27, 1796, pending the formation of the special high court and the preparation of the indictment. The President of the Court was Gandon, and he was aided by a bench of five other judges as well as by two supplementary judges. The public prosecutors were Vieillart and Bailly. There was a jury of sixteen. Forty-seven prisoners in all were presented to the court—each guarded by two gendarmes,

[1] Some interesting light has been shed on judicial procedure at this time by Sir Charles Oman's little study of *The Lyons Mail* (1945). The celebrated highway crime was attracting attention in Paris just at the time of Babeuf's plot ; it happened on April 27, 1796.

while a large body of troops surrounded the court buildings. The public which attended the trial consisted
almost entirely of Babouvist sympathizers, who loudly
applauded the prisoners' statements ; but Paris—and
France as a whole—soon lost interest in the tedious
proceedings.

The chief defence was put up by Babeuf himself, and
by Buonarroti and Germain. Darthé made only one
speech at the beginning of the proceedings, in which he
refused to recognize the jurisdiction of the court, and then
remained silent. His solitary speech, delivered in the
finest rhetorical form, expressed his total lack of regret
for his own fate now that France, liberty and all that he
valued were submitted to so much degradation.

The prosecution made the strategic mistake of violently
overstating its case. It tried to present the conspirators
as unnatural monsters, the latest manifestation of that
diabolical faction which had perpetrated one atrocity
after another, from the fall of the Bastille to the fall of
Robespierre. It thus put itself and the Government on
the side of opposition to all the most dramatic, romantic
and already almost legendary popular achievements of
the Revolution as a whole. It appealed against everything that meant democracy. Its chief witnesses were
particularly despicable specimens like the spy Grisel, who
were least calculated to arouse any sympathy from the
public. To secure a witness like Grisel, the prosecution
had to evade the law that a denunciator could not be
heard in cases where he could directly profit by denunciation. The court therefore ruled that his statement had
been a " revelation " because made to Carnot, and not a
" denunciation " within the meaning of the law, which
brought derision on the whole proceedings.

The burden of the indictment was that the accused
had formed a conspiracy with the aim of " usurping

sovereignty " in the State. The strategy of the defence
was to accept gladly all the seized documents as authenti-
cally their own, and at first Babeuf and the ringleaders
were tempted to proclaim themselves proud to have taken
the initiative in plotting to overthrow so rotten a régime.
But it was argued—especially by those less directly im-
plicated—that to admit the fact of conspiracy would
jeopardize the defence unnecessarily. According to
Buonarroti it was therefore agreed that formal conspiracy
should be denied, but should be " hypothetically "
justified. This curious line of defence produced equally
curious results. The accused made no attempt to hide
their beliefs, but denied formal conspiracy. They seized
every opportunity to prolong the trial by lengthy speeches
and to expound again and again their beliefs to an appre-
ciative audience. At moments of crisis they would break
into lines of the *Marseillaise*, led by Sophie Lapierre of
the Bains-Chinois, and ended each day's session by singing
republican hymns. Two soldiers summoned as witnesses
bowed to the prisoners and greeted them with revolutionary songs. The interrogation of Babeuf alone lasted
nine sessions. He used it to glorify the Constitution of
1793 which he declared had been usurped by the Directory ; to justify the right of insurrection in such circumstances ; and to explain that his ideals were the rule of
equality and the happiness of the people. The defence
of Buonarroti, which is recorded at length in his own
memoirs, followed similar lines. These disorderly proceedings and the bravery and irrepressibility of the
prisoners aroused public sympathy.

The judges were inordinately patient in face of the
obstreperous and " filibustering " tactics employed by the
accused. The appearance of Grisel as a witness, for
example, provoked the most violent scenes from the
prisoners. There is evidence that the conspirators con-

spired even in their cells and in the court-room. They apportioned duties to each of their leaders—one to heckle witnesses, one to arrange interjections in the speeches of the prosecution, and so on. Babeuf smuggled out messages in code, arranging for the attempt to rescue the prisoners. They protested at every opportunity—against the clerks recording the proceedings, against people present in the court-room, and of course against all witnesses for the prosecution. They exploited to the full the overstatements of the prosecution's case ; and perhaps it was one success of their own violent tactics to have provoked the prosecution into this major strategic error. One quotation from the charge of Vieillart, for the prosecution, will illustrate this error which was so valuable to the defence.

> Dans le bouleversement des éléments sociaux, ces mélanges impurs ont fermenté ; et de leur sein est éclos une espèce d'êtres malfaisants, monstres jusque-là inconnus dans ces climats, et que le ciel même semblait avoir épargnés à la terre ; ils se proclamaient *les patriotes*, et ils ont déchiré, mutilé, dévoré la Patrie !
> . . . Fils de l'anarchie, nés dans son sein, élevés dans ses bras, leur instinct ne connaît pas d'autre élément. Ils l'appellent sans cesse, ils ne sourient qu'à elle. L'ordre, l'ordre, voeu et besoin de tous les êtres sensibles, est, pour ceux-ci, un tourment. Ils frémissent à son aspect ; ils rugissent de joie quand la tempête approche, ils se précipitent au milieu des désordres publics avec le cri d'un féroce plaisir. La nuit affreuse qui a couvert la France de carnage, à l'épouvantable époque de la Terreur, est l'objet continuel de tous leurs regrets. . . . Tout moyen pour arriver à leur but leur paraît également bon : dévaster, égorger jusqu'à ce que leur affreux système surnage sur un mer de sang : voilà leur doctrine.

The argument of the defence, that because the existing régime was a usurpation the conspiracy was completely justifiable, turned the edge of the whole trial. The prosecution strove to avoid this second issue, and to restrict the issues to the mere facts of the conspiracy—but without complete success. Such was the triumph of the Babouvists' strategy of defence. When a political trial becomes—as all are wont to do—a trial of a régime rather than of individual men, it rapidly gets beyond the control of the prosecution and the initiative falls to the defence. This the men of Vichy found at Riom in 1943, and their successors found too, in 1945, in the trials of Marshal Pétain, Laval and Darnand.

Before long the prosecution found itself outmanœuvred by the skill of Babeuf and his colleagues in turning every question into a defence of the Constitution of 1793 and an indictment of the Directory. It was often at a loss for an answer to their telling retorts and forceful arguments. The complete defence of Babeuf occupied four days. In textual form, left by him for later publication, it covers more than three hundred pages. Though as verbose and rhetorical as ever, it comprised a re-exposition of his doctrines as well as a vindication of his own acts. He read from a written statement of some two hundred folio pages, and attempted to refute in detail the charges levied by the prosecution. In the course of it he provided a summary of his doctrine as succinct and apposite as any he ever wrote. " I have ventured", he said, " to conceive and preach this doctrine " :

The natural right of men and their destiny is to be happy and free. Society is established to guarantee more securely for each member his natural right and destiny. When these natural rights are not secured for all, the social contract is broken. To prevent the social contract being broken, there must be some sanction. This sanction can reside only in the right of each citizen to watch over its infringements, to denounce them to all other members, to be first in resisting oppression, and to exhort other members to resist. Hence is derived the inviolable, unlimited and individual right to think, reflect, communicate one's thoughts and reflections to others. . . ."

He pleaded, in short, his *philosophe* orthodoxy : that his speeches and writings contained no principles that could not already be found in the most venerated precursors of the Revolution—in Rousseau, Mably, Morelly, Diderot.

The trial was brought to a close only by the bench insisting that the substantial question put to the jury should be simply whether or not the accused had conspired, " with intention to conspire ", so excluding all question of justification for the conspiracy. Only on this issue, indeed, could any clear verdict be given ; and on this the verdict was a foregone conclusion, since abundant documentary evidence of the facts was available. Three or four of the jury of sixteen were favourable to the accused, and only nine of the prisoners were fully convicted. Of these nine, " extenuating circumstances " were allowed to cover seven, so that only Babeuf and Darthé remained liable to the death penalty. On the announcement of the death sentence for Darthé and Babeuf, and transportation for the other seven, a great uproar occurred. Babeuf and Darthé stabbed themselves with daggers; but the daggers, being clumsy homemade ones, failed to kill them. After a night of agony in their cells, the two men were dragged already dying to the guillotine. Both died with conspicuous courage, and their bodies were recovered and buried reverently in a field nearby by their local supporters.

There is an epilogue to the personal story of Babeuf. He left a wife and three sons who were looked after, as promised, by the only well-to-do Babouvist conspirator, Félix Le Pelletier. The eldest son Robert, rechristened Émile, he actually adopted. This son seems to have inherited many of his father's characteristics and beliefs. He joined the Spanish nationalists in the war of independence some years later, and heard that the spy, Grisel, was also in Spain. He ferreted him out and challenged him to a duel. It was a duel to the death—the death of Grisel. In other ways, too, Émile made it a mission of his life to vindicate his father's honour and sustain the tradition. He too ran a Jacobin journal in Paris, which had to be suppressed by the police. He served under the Emperor Napoleon, and after Waterloo migrated to America where he died some years later. Of the other two sons, one was killed in battle in 1814, the other committed suicide in 1815. Émile's only son, Louis Pierre, led a respectable life as a *fonctionnaire* and died in 1871, just before the outbreak of the Paris Commune which drew so much force from the ideas of his grandfather. The family of Babeuf died out at the moment when the Babouvist legend reached its climax—a fitting sequel to the personal fate of its founder. Émile, in a mass of personal notes which he left, strove to vindicate his father. He added thereby to a story vivid and dramatic enough in all conscience, and started on its course the highly decorated legend which was to pass into the nineteenth century through the pen and the career of Philippe Buonarroti.

Buonarroti is a figure in the legend of Babouvism second in interest only to Babeuf himself. A descendant of Michelangelo, he came of a well-to-do noble family of Tuscany, and a good career lay open to him in Italy.

He studied law at Paris and steeped himself in the writings of the French *philosophes*, particularly Rousseau. But his open atheism forced him to move to Corsica in 1789, where he became acquainted with the Bonaparte family and with Napoleon personally. There his republicanism was better appreciated, and there he served the republican governments until the fall of Robespierre. He was made a French citizen by the Convention in 1793 and held several important administrative and propagandist posts. Imprisoned after Robespierre's fall in 1794, he fell in with the Babouvists and henceforth, as will be seen, prison life was the normal *milieu* for the growth of Babouvism. Cut off from his wife, family and fortune in Italy, he found another wife and family—and other fortunes—in France. For his share in the Babeuf Plot he was imprisoned, but by 1806 he was living—still under police supervision—in Geneva, the favourite resort of so many exiles. Forced to earn his living in exile, he drifted permanently into the ranks of the *révolutionnaires de métier*, from which even his potentially profitable connections with Bonaparte did not seduce him. By 1812 he was engaged in a plot against Napoleon, whose monarchical form of government he regarded as a complete betrayal of revolutionary and republican ideals.

After the Bourbon restoration of 1815 he concerned himself more with the liberation and unification of his native Italy than with France. This preoccupation brought him into contact with Mazzini, the Carbonari and the Young Italy movement. He insisted that republicanism must be purely international in organization and ideals, in which he was at cross-purposes with the intense nationalism of Mazzini; and his influence on Italian revolutionary movements is more on the technique of conspiracy and revolution than on the ideology of republicanism. He favoured using Freemasonry as a façade for conspiracy, and tried to found a Society of *Sublimes-Maîtres-Parfaits*, or revolutionary *élite*. The old Secret Directory of Babeuf cast a long shadow on the revolutionary movements of the 1820's.

In France, however, his name was not forgotten. The rule of the returned *émigrés* in France, under Louis XVIII and still more under Charles X, produced conditions in which underground conspiracies were the only recourse left to moderate liberals and men who clung to the revolutionary ideals. The Carbonari, in which Buonarroti became a leading figure, had after 1821 its French counterpart in the *Charbonnerie française*. The aim of this secret society was to give back to the French nation " the free exercise of the right to choose its sovereign ". Amid such conditions the repute of Buonarroti spread, and young revolutionaries everywhere began to pay attention to the veteran conspirator whose name was linked with pre-Napoleonic days.

The idea that the liberal secret societies of the Restoration period were perpetuating the tradition of Babouvist plots was spread most actively by the royalist ministries themselves. Villèle was particularly skilful at manufacturing " Red scares " in order to present the King and himself as the saviours of social order. It was the monarchists who tarred Liberals with a Babouvist brush. When four sergeants of La Rochelle tried to enrol their men in a secret society they were condemned to death, and the Public Prosecutor denounced " this vast conspiracy against social order, against the families of citizens, which threatened to plunge them once more into all the horrors of anarchy." It was the Ultras who accused Liberals of wanting " democracy ", the " Agrarian Law ", and *Communauté des biens*.

From Geneva Buonarroti exerted a long-range attraction on men thus repressed. One of his music pupils who was also a member of the *Charbonnerie*, Alexandre Andryane, has left this picture of him in Geneva :

> Il est à Genève un vieillard qui, depuis long-temps, excite ma curiosité. Dès les premiers moments que je le rencontrai, sa tournure, sa mise, sa démarche me frappèrent : un chapeau à larges bords couvre sa blanche chevelure ; son front est vaste et bombé ; ses yeux, surmontés de sourcils touffus, sont vifs et brillent souvent au milieu des larges verres de ses lunettes de fer ; sa figure caractérisée lui donne un aspect vénérable et, quoique sa tête soit inclinée sur sa poitrine et que ses épaules soient voûtées, on voit à son col nerveux, à sa charpente osseuse, que la vigueur et la force furent un jour l'apanage de cet homme que les traverses de la vie doivent avoir usé plus que l'âge.
>
> Été comme hiver, il porte le même habit, le même gilet à la Robespierre, les mêmes culottes noires qui ne joignent pas tout à fait ses demi-bottes à l'écuyère, costume assez étrange par lui-même et qui suffirait seul pour le faire remarquer si quelque chose de fier et d'original ne vous forçait à jeter les yeux sur ce sexagénaire qui vous croise à chaque instant dans les rues étroites de Genève, un livre de musique sous le bras, en passant près de vous d'un air grave, préoccupé et mystérieux.[1]

In 1823 Buonarroti left Geneva and moved to the Netherlands. Here he fulfilled the pledge he had made to Darthé and Babeuf in the court-room of Vendôme before their condemnation. He had promised " to avenge their memory, by publishing an exact account of our common intentions, which the spirit of party had so

---

[1] Alexandre Andryane : *Souvenirs de Genève, complément des Mémoires d'un prisonnier d'État.* Vol. I, pp. 137–8.

strangely disfigured ". His great two-volume documentary work was published in Brussels in 1828 : the *Conspiration pour l'Égalité dite de Babeuf.* It was a mixture of personal memoirs and documents. He placed on record the inside story of the Plot, trial and death of Babeuf for study not only by historians but also by future revolutionaries. It was a potent factor in the growth of the legend. The *mystique* of Babouvism was launched by the actual life, trial and death of Babeuf. The young man of thirty-seven who died so flamboyantly for his ideals inevitably inspired devotion and affection in his disciples who survived. But it would have remained a tragic and picturesque historical incident—one among many others in the heroic years after 1789—had there not been this timely reminder of the story in Buonarroti's book.

Much of the book's significance lies in its timing. The crescendo of reaction in Europe between 1815 and 1830 meant that by the 1830's men were ready to seize upon any interpretation of the great French Revolution which helped to explain the triumph of reaction and the frustration of democracy. In the writings of Babeuf and the story of the Plot there lay, ready to hand, just such an interpretation. The events of 1796 had been the turning-point. The Thermidorian reaction, leading straight to the rule of Bonaparte whose Italian campaign began in that year, had marked the end of serious attempts to push revolutionary ideals to their natural and logical conclusion. The Revolution had ended not in 1795 but in 1796. The foiled conspiracy had been the last flicker of hope that liberty and equality would find realization as operative ideals ; its failure meant that they had become meaningless shibboleths.

Although Babouvism played little or no part in the actual Revolution of 1830, which replaced Charles X by Louis Philippe, the July Revolution prepared the ground

for the first great revival of Babouvism. It was again the
more conservative forces which triumphed in 1830 : the
wealthier *bourgeoisie* used the change to entrench themselves in political power. To the Jacobins and the new
Socialist groups it was a second great betrayal, comparable
to 1796. The oppressiveness of the régime in the late
1830's created a new generation of underground conspiracies and secret societies ; and now it was the radical
Republicans and Socialists who were the chief recruits for
such activity. The revolutionaries of the July Monarchy,
working in conditions that were new, strove to link their
own efforts to the epic story of the Babouvists, and so
emphasize the direct continuity of the revolutionary tradition. The Jacobins, who had been uneasy allies of the
Babouvists in 1796, found solidarity with them again in
the cry for " Bread and the Constitution of 1793".

Now, too, there was a direct link between the new secret
societies and the old in the person and the writing of
Philippe Buonarroti. The July Revolution in 1830 had
allowed him to return to France, and in that year his
book made its first appearance in a French edition. His
aim was to make Paris once again the centre and head-
quarters of all European revolutions. The book of the
famous conspirator became the text-book and almost the
breviary of the new generation of young Parisian revolutionaries. The counsel he gave to the young French
democrats was, " The *carrière des conspirations* is the most
difficult but the most worthy of all : consider well before
entering it." Conspiracy was a calling for the expert as
well as for the enthusiast. He gave advice on how to get
into relations with the populace, and advised caution in
planning action. He tried to discourage the rising at
Lyons in 1834, but became associated with it because his
name appeared in the list of its defenders. At the same
time he preserved his international connections. He

became a revered correspondent of all the secret societies in Germany ; remained an active force in the Carbonari ; and in France he grouped around him a cluster of personal disciples. These were men like Andryane, to whom he taught Italian and music as well as politics ; the young Charles Teste, who spent his life organizing resistance to the hated Monarchy ; and Voyer d'Argenson, who created a great sensation in the Chamber by preaching not only equality of political rights but also *égalité des conditions sociales.*

Still the conservative forces were helping to strengthen the legend of Babouvism by denouncing all republicans as a " Red menace " to law and order. The exaggeration with which the prosecution had attacked the Babouvists in 1796, and the Bourbon monarchists had condemned Liberals before 1830, was now repeated in the 1830's. The Jacobin bogy haunted the governing and propertied classes throughout the first half of the nineteenth century as persistently as the menace of Bolshevism haunted their counterparts in the first half of the twentieth century ; and it was half-identified with Babouvism. And all " Babouvists " were notoriously anarchists and atheists, cut-throat revolutionaries who were the enemies of society, and of all decency. From being the " lunatic fringe " of the Jacobins, the Babouvists came to be regarded more and more—as indeed they had been—the logical exponents of a thoroughgoing Jacobinism, revealing, it was claimed, the full horribleness of the whole creed because they drew from it its natural consequences.[1] They came to be viewed, by revolutionaries and reactionaries alike, as the Trotskyites of Jacobinism.

Apart from this help which the Babeuf legend received

---

[1] Thus the anonymous pamphlet, *Lyon et Paris en avril 1834,* spoke of the " Republicans of to-day wanting, like Babeuf and Robespierre, to level all conditions and all fortunes." Fear of the guillotine becoming again " the great leveller " was still an active bogy.

D

from the conservatives, other conditions favoured its growth. The simplicity of Babouvism gave it a powerful appeal in popular propaganda during the 1830's. Workers imprisoned for their part in riots and strikes met, in prison, readers and friends of Buonarroti. To aggrieved men the simplicity of the Babouvist solution held great attractions. Societies not by nature communistic found in it telling propaganda. The Society of the Rights of Man, Jacobin but not Babouvist in ideology, found it convenient when appealing for working-class support to conjure up a future régime in which the property of the rich would be levelled out. Buonarroti's book was fast spreading its influence. In 1836 the English Chartist leader, Bronterre O'Brien, produced an abridged English version of it. In 1842 a further abridged version appeared in French, followed by others in 1849 and 1850. Throughout the turbulent decades 1828–48, the legend of Babeuf's Plot was seeping into European revolutionary literature ; and Buonarroti's influence, both personal and literary, was steadily growing.

A turning-point in the fortunes of the legend seems to have come in 1834. The industrial revolution and the conservative middle-class rule of Louis Philippe were, in interaction, driving sections of the distressed industrial workers towards thoughts of socialism. The striking and widening gulf between rich and poor was preparing the soil for Babouvist ideas of equality. In 1834 republican societies were made illegal and driven underground. Laws of 1835 restricting the Press strengthened the hands of those who urged secret conspiracy as the only effective political weapon. Babouvist influence can be traced in the manifestos and declarations of such bodies as the *Légions révolutionnaires* in 1835 and 1836, in the rules and organization of the *Familles* and the *Phalanges démocratiques* and similar societies. Until 1841 at least, Babouvist ideas of conspiracy and equality dominated these societies. Thereafter the ideas of Saint-Simon, Fourier and Cabet tended to take their place. Buonarroti died in 1837.

There are countless echoes of the Babeuf Plot in the famous revolt of *Les Saisons* in 1839. The Society of the Seasons was run by Blanqui, Barbès and Martin Bernard —all in some degree disciples of Babouvism and of Robespierrism. It was concerned to unite the many secret republican societies and to mobilize them for a conspiracy on the lines of Babeuf's. It organized its members into groups of six (" weeks "), each of which was commanded by a " Sunday " ; four weeks formed a " month " under the orders of a " July ", three months a " season ", commanded by a " Spring ", and four seasons a " year ", directed by a special revolutionary agent. On May 12, 1839 some 600 or 700 insurgents, so organized, pillaged the armourers' stores in the districts of Saint Denis and Saint Martin in Paris and threw up the barricades. That evening the leaders were arrested, and the plot collapsed. Although their trial—like most political trials of this period—gave the insurgents a further opportunity to expound their theories and seek martyrdom in the approved Babouvist fashion, it was as complete a failure as its prototype of 1796. Barbès and Blanqui were condemned to death, but the sentence was commuted to one of imprisonment. Was Louis Philippe resolved to avoid making any further martyrs in the manner of Babeuf? Certainly Barbès, when sentenced, invoked as his patrons and predecessors Saint Just, Robespierre, Couthon and Babeuf. It was in the decade of the 1830's that the conception of Babeuf as the first socialist martyr took a firm hold on the imagination of the French working classes and the republican parties.

Yet the influence of Babouvism even on the republican parties of this period should not be exaggerated. One whole section of French republicans was dominated by American ideas rather than by French—looking more to 1776 than to 1789 for their inspiration. Many movements were concerned ideologically only with parliamentary action and with purely political rights—such as the *Association pour la liberté de la presse.* The Jacobins looked back more to 1793 than to 1796. The *Société des Droits de l'Homme* might find it convenient to use Babouvist language, but its origins and purpose were by no means Babouvist. Similarly in organization : it established a central committee of eleven elected members, and " sections " each of ten to twenty members distributed by *arrondissements.* But the forms of organization which secret societies adopted were dictated more by conditions than by precedents ; and necessity was a harder, more impressive, master than even Buonarroti. The *Société des Amis du Peuple* was in the direct tradition of Marat, and included men like Auguste Blanqui who learnt much of his revolutionary methods from Babeuf and Buonarroti. But it borrowed little that was doctrinal from Babouvism. Saint-Simon was more its ideological master. It is not in detail that the influence of Babouvism should be sought. Its eternal basis was desperation and hunger. As Espinas remarked in his sympathetic study of Babouvism, *Le bonheur que Babeuf rêve pour l'humanité, c'est d'être sûr de ne pas mourir de faim* ; and of the Babouvists of any age it is true that *leur socialisme est le cri de l'estomac.*

It is for this reason that the growing prosperity of Louis Philippe's reign brought, in the 1840's, a temporary lull in the growth of Babouvist influence in France. The increase of wealth removed the fear of want ; and only when the disproportionate distribution of this wealth fed still further grievances was the stage set for the revolution of 1848. Just as the years between 1828 and 1840 saw the first resurgence of the Babouvist legend, so the years

1848–52 saw a revival of Babouvism in the circumstances of growing political discontent and the accumulating evidence that no drastic social reforms could be expected from the *bourgeoisie*. The revolution of 1848 which set up the Second French Republic, and brought a new concern for social problems in the experiment of " National workshops " inspired by Louis Blanc, gave rise to a renewed interest in egalitarian and Babouvist ideas. The legend thrived on the repeated failure of French governments to deal with the social problems inherent in the spread of industrialism. It jostled with new movements, virtually independent in origin, which were tending in the same direction : with Saint-Simonism, the Icarian brand of communism promoted by Cabet, and the Marxist communism of Karl Marx and Friedrich Engels, who published their *Communist Manifesto* in 1848. Under the Second Republic, there were some 145 political clubs in Paris and the Paris neighbourhood, and some of them became the home and the hotbed of the old school of *révolutionnaires de métier*, of whom Blanqui was fast becoming the idol. Theirs was the tradition of the barricades and resistance *à outrance*. Babouvism found a new organ of propaganda in *L'Humanitaire*.

On two men of this period Babouvism exerted a certain, though somewhat intangible, influence. Both deserve mention because both moved like Babeuf from the realm of mere theory and academic agitation to the realm of practical experiments. They are Louis Blanc and Étienne Cabet. Louis Blanc launched in 1848 the ill-fated experiment in " National workshops ", and Cabet founded an experimental communistic colony in America on lines similar to Robert Owen's " New Harmony ". How much if anything did these experiments owe to the *mystique* of Babouvism ?

In the decrees prepared ready for enforcement after a

successful *coup*, the conspirators had foreshadowed the
setting up of what would have been, in effect, national
workshops.   Blanc, like Babeuf, was inspired with the
need to abandon airy theories for consideration of the
concrete means by which they can be reduced to practical
experiment.   He saw that socialism must be a matter of
everyday politics.   And for him, as for Babeuf, " whatever
is, is wrong ".   The test of the Republic and of democracy
is a social test :   does it guarantee to the worker his *droit
au travail* ?   To do so, it must organize work, provide
work ;   and this it can best do in national workshops,
which would eventually be run democratically by the
workers themselves.   Like Babeuf he writes sometimes of
equality of reward for labour, at other times of remunera-
tion according to function, and at others of distribution
according to needs.   His teaching was not clear, and the
actual experiment in national workshops, which utterly
failed, was not—as he protested—in accordance with his
ideas.   But in so far as he paid homage to rigid egalitarian
ideas, he seems to have been partly influenced by his
regard for Babouvism.   Perhaps his essential views are
expressed most clearly in his *Catéchisme des Socialistes*, published in 1849.   It is written in the form of catechism :

> *D.*—Qu'est-ce que l'égalité ?
>
> *R.*—C'est, pour tous les hommes, *l'égal* développe-
> ment de leurs facultés *inégales*, et *l'égale* satisfac-
> tion de leurs besoins *inégaux*. . . .
>
> *D.*—L'égalité, selon vous, n'est donc que la propor-
> tionnalité ?
>
> *R.*—Certainement, et elle n'existera d'une manière
> véritable que lorsque chacun, d'après la loi
> écrite en quelque sorte dans son organisation
> par Dieu lui-même, *produira selon ses facultés et
> consommera selon ses besoins*. . . .

D.—Qu'est-ce que la fraternité ?
R.—C'est l'égalité consacrée, positive, sanctifiée et maintenue par l'amour.

The story of Étienne Cabet is no more conclusive. His *Voyage en Icarie* for which he is famous appeared in 1842— in the same decade as Louis Blanc's *L'Organisation du Travail.* It is the description of a Utopia, a clean, clinical, scientific, communistic Utopia, run by democratically elected technicians. The State is run to promote the happiness of every citizen through ensuring his material and spiritual welfare. The State, being based on the general will of the whole community, knows no limits to its sphere of action : it is omnicompetent, omnipresent and totalitarian. Icarian society knows no classes or privileges. It is egalitarian. There are no property, money or trading. All work equally for the community and are equally rewarded. The connection between Cabet and the Babouvists is close. He belonged to the *Charbonnerie* at the time when Buonarroti was most influential in it ; he was intimate with d'Argenson, one of Buonarroti's most ardent disciples ; and he read Buonarroti's book on the Babeuf Plot. It made little impression on him at first—he read it chiefly for the celebrity of its author. He was therefore subject to both the personal and the literary influence of the veteran conspirator. But the great amount of ink which has been spent on trying to assess the precise sources of his ideas is largely wasted. None—least of all a man himself— can assess exactly where and when he picked up this idea or that. A man's views and ideals are nearly always a peculiar amalgam of conscious and unconscious borrowings from others, combined with his own reflections on them and blended to suit his own circumstances, temperament and predilections. Suffice to say that Cabet's bias towards Utopian communism and doctrinaire equality

was strengthened, at least, by his early and close association with the Babouvists. In his own *Histoire populaire de
la Révolution Française* he passed unfavourable judgments
on Babeuf and the Conspiracy ; and this appeared in
1839—the same year as his first edition of the *Voyage en
Icarie* and as Louis Blanc's first draft of *L'Organisation du
Travail*. It is notably, also, the year of the revolt of *Les
Saisons*, led by Blanqui and Barbès, against the government
of Louis Philippe. Again it was a period when the gulf
between reality and men's vision of the possible produced
on the one hand utopian dreams and on the other political
agitation and revolt. Similarity of conditions can explain
the similarity between Cabet and the Babouvists without
presupposing direct borrowing of ideas. All were engaged
in the work of the various republican societies which were
so active under the July Monarchy ; and these activities
aroused a conservative opposition which, as usual, lumped
all agitators together as Jacobins and Babouvists.

The history of the Icarian community which was established in America is long and intriguing. It has been ably
told by M. Jules Prudhommeaux in his *Histoire de la
Communauté Icarienne*. Cabet first secured a grant of land
in Texas in 1847, but when yellow fever broke out in the
community it migrated to Nauvoo in Illinois, where some
1,500 Icarians gathered. But when dissension also broke
out, many disillusioned Icarians returned to France. It
failed as a social experiment, and the few offshoots of it
which lingered on may have had some local influence but
had no general importance. Even so, it was October
1898 before the last Icarian group at Corning was
declared finally dissolved by a judge of Iowa.

The *Communist Manifesto* of Marx and Engels was
written against the background of these communistic
ideas which they christened Utopian. The first number

of the *Communist Journal*, which appeared in London in September 1847, opened with a criticism of Cabet's projected American colony. So, too, Marx was critical of Babeuf. " To take Babeuf as the theoretical exponent of communism ", he declared irritably on one occasion, " could only have entered the head of a Berlin schoolmaster." But in 1845 he allowed, accurately enough, the place of Babeuf in socialist thought, and drew the conclusion we might expect. " The most logical communists (in England, the Levellers, and in France, Babeuf, Buonarroti, and so forth) are the first to stress social questions. In *Gracchus Babeuf et la conjuration des égaux* written by Babeuf's friend and comrade, Buonarroti, we read how these republicans learned by practical experience that, even if such ' social questions ' as monarchy versus republic could be settled, this would not solve one single ' social question ' in the proletarian sense of the words." In the activities of the later Babouvists, particularly of Buonarroti and Blanqui, Marx and Engels saw this original Utopian communism finding, at last, its true proletarian level.

In the *Communist Manifesto* Marx and Engels mentioned Babeuf and the legend of Babouvism as the French precursors of their own movement ; of the insurgence of the proletariat against bourgeois society.

> We do not here refer to that literature which, in every great modern revolution, has always given voice to the demands of the proletariat, such as the writings of Babeuf and others. The first direct attempts of the proletariat to attain its own ends, made in times of universal excitement when feudal society was being overthrown, these attempts necessarily failed, owing to the then undeveloped state of the proletariat, as well as to the economic conditions

D*

for its emancipation, conditions that had yet to be produced, and could be produced by the impending bourgeois epoch alone. The revolutionary literature that accompanied these first movements of the proletariat had necessarily a reactionary character. It inculcated universal asceticism and social levelling in its crudest forms.

Although they wrote in disparaging terms of Babouvism, the communist programme which they expounded in the *Manifesto* has much in common with that of Babeuf. It included the following :

1. Abolition of property in land and application of all rents of land to public purposes.
2. A heavy progressive or graduated income tax.
3. Abolition of all rights of inheritance.
4. Confiscation of the property of all emigrants and rebels.
5. Centralization of credit in the hands of the State, by means of a national bank, with State capital and an exclusive monopoly.
6. Centralization of the means of communication and transport in the hands of the State.
7. Extension of factories and instruments of production owned by the State : the bringing into cultivation of waste lands, and the improvement of the soil generally in accordance with a common plan.
8. Equal obligation of all to work. Establishment of industrial armies, especially for agriculture.

Each of these points was substantially included in Babeuf's writings and in the plans of the conspirators for effecting the social revolution after their *coup d'état*. And elsewhere Marx admitted more generously than in the *Manifesto* his debt to Babeuf. He wrote :

The French Revolution gave birth to notions which went beyond the ideas of the established state of things. The revolutionary movement, which in 1789, with the *Cercle Social*, which found its main representatives in the course of its evolution, Leclerc and Roux, and finished with the conspiracy of Babeuf, gave birth to the Communist notions which Buonarroti, friend of Babeuf, re-introduced into France after the Revolution of 1830. This idea, enhanced by its consequences, is the idea of the new state of things.

And Engels declared that one of the merits of Babeuf was to have drawn the " final conclusion from the idea of equality embodied in the Constitution of 1793 ".

In 1851, the year when Victorian England celebrated the hey-day of its material prosperity by the Great Exhibition at the Crystal Palace, and Louis Napoleon, President of the Second French Republic, again frustrated the hopes of French republicans by the *coup d'état* which established the Second Empire, a *Banquet des Égaux* was held in London. The diners embodied all the ideas of Babeuf in a joint profession of faith ; but that was in February, and by December the Second Republic had gone the way of the first—trampled under the heel of a Bonaparte.

The political clubs and revolutionary activities in France of these years (1848–52) were marked by one peculiarity : their most active and extremist members were recruited from the older generation. The younger men and women attended societies and political meetings to learn about politics. They were the enthusiastic and energetic products of universal suffrage and political republicanism, and their interests were more in political than in social reforms. The older generation, trained in secret conspiracy, were the products of the Carbonari movements and the secret societies of the Restoration period and the July Monarchy. It was this middle-aged minority which clung to the older tradition of the barricades and to the vocabulary of 1793 ; it was they who had learned about the Great Revolution from men like Buonarroti. Only a minority of the younger generation inherited or acquired these habits, and from the *conspirateurs de métier* like Blanqui and Barbès learnt at first hand how to fight for republicanism underground against the totalitarian dictatorship of Napoleon III. The more moderate liberal republicans were able, after 1860, to voice their views in Parliament and the Press. The old revolutionaries still clung to the time-honoured (if also time-discredited) methods of secret conspiracy, search for a revolutionary *élite*, and devotion to study of the precise revolutionary technique which would at last yield certain success. Their normal home was still prison, where most of them spent a very considerable portion of their lives.

Nor were these middle-aged revolutionaries proletarian. Auguste Blanqui himself was the son of a Napoleonic *fonctionnaire*. For him, as for Buonarroti, legal studies were a prelude to illegal activities. Each new revolution gave him a fresh opportunity for active conspiracy which he seized with unfailing enthusiasm. He was little interested in more than the first part of Babeuf's programme—the seizure of power and the procedure for a *coup de main*. He continued, for instance, a tactic which the Babouvists had evolved and which Buonarroti had employed in 1814 known as " invisible manœuvres ". Grouped in tens under a leader who alone was in touch with the central organization, the conspirators would meet and march together in the midst of a holiday crowd, their disciplined formation passing unnoticed in the crowd.

After the establishment of the Government of National Defence on September 4, 1870, when the Second Empire had gone down in defeat at Sedan, this veteran of the barricades (he was then sixty-five and had already spent twenty-eight years in prison) at once established a club and a journal with the title *La Patrie en Danger*. For attempting to seize power the next month, he was condemned to death (for the second time in his life) and only the outbreak of the Paris Commune in March 1871 saved him. It also gave him his one real chance of power, for he was taken into the government of the Commune, in the creation of which his disciples played a considerable part. After the crushing of the Commune by Thiers he was condemned to transportation which was commuted to imprisonment. In 1879, the year of the Republican Party triumph, he was elected Deputy for Bordeaux. He might even yet have played some part in the evolution of the Third Republic, but he died suddenly in 1881. He died—appropriately enough—of apoplexy, after addressing a revolutionary meeting, on New Year's Day. The age of apoplectic politics was passing away, and Blanqui was already a figure from a half-forgotten age.

The belief in professional, expert revolutionaries, acting as a small *élite* and able to mobilize only two or three thousand militant followers in a select conspiracy, died hard. Blanqui, the most complete and logical exponent of this belief, was the spokesman of the uprooted intellectuals and the *déclassé bourgeois* who, in the mid-nineteenth century, were the true followers of the Babouvist tradition. His revolutionary strategy was based on this belief. Thinking even before Marx in terms of " the Industrial Revolution " and " dictatorship of the proletariat "—phrases which he coined—he analysed the situation thus : the masses (or proletariat) are uneducated and must be led by the educated, revolutionary section of the

middle classes. These can only be trained in the appropriate technique in revolutionary Paris ; therefore all
revolution must start from barricades in the Paris streets,
erected under the guidance of the expert revolutionaries.
In 1917 Lenin stated the Marxist objection to, and diver-
gence from, this old tradition.

> Insurrection must be based not on a plot, not on a
> party, but on the advanced class. That is the first
> point. Insurrection must be based on the revolu-
> tionary drive of the whole people. That is the second
> point. Insurrection must break out at the climax of
> the ascending revolution. That is the third point.
> It is by these three conditions that Marxism is dis-
> tinguished from Blanquism.

After 1871, the tide of revolutionary movements forked
more clearly and sharply into Socialist organization acting
through trade unionism and parliamentary parties on the
one hand, and Marxist Communism, at times using similar
methods but more impatiently seeking drastic revolution,
on the other. The tradition of Babeuf, Buonarroti and
Blanqui fitted comfortably into neither stream. Perpetual
exile and imprisonment had proved an unfruitful fate for
revolutionaries, and more thorough preparation, more
patient planning and organization, were clearly called for
rather than reckless revolts and untimely conspiracies.
Even in 1848 many progressive minds had seen the futility
of Blanquist methods. Louis Blanc confined himself to
more practical objectives. And a liberal democrat like
de Tocqueville was shocked by the appearance of Blanqui
in the Chamber in May 1848.

> His cheeks were haggard and emaciate, his lips
> vivid, his appearance sickly, sinister and unclean ; a
> dirty pallor, the aspect of a rotting corpse, no visible

linen, an old black frock-coat tightly draping ravaged limbs, he seemed to have spent his life in a sewer, from which he had just emerged.

After 1871 this tradition, outmoded in western Europe, found a home further east ; and it is noteworthy that towards the end of his life Blanqui was contributing to Tkatchev's *Nabat*, the organ of the Narodnaia Volya, the Russian nihilist party.

Meanwhile, as already suggested, the anti-Babouvists made their own peculiar contribution to the growth of the legend. The more revolutionaries seized upon Babeuf as a symbol and made the Babouvist plot the fountain-head of modern communism, the more conservatives came to regard Babeuf as his prosecutors had tried to depict him. The Babouvists became cut-throats and ruffians, the scum of society whose pernicious influence still haunted and agitated men's minds in the alarming movements of socialism and communism. This reactionary contribution to the legend was crystallized in Édouard Fleury's biography of Babeuf, published significantly in 1851, the year of Napoleon's *coup d'état*.[1] The hero and martyr of the Left became, logically enough, the bogy and *bête-noire* of the Right. Written in a tone of hatred and sarcasm, Fleury's book presented Babeuf as the ringleader of a gang of cut-throats, a reckless, hypocritical doctrinaire, seeking to improve his own fortunes by the overthrow of society. He overlooked no means of discrediting him, although admitting his fanaticism and his bravery at the end. He saw in the legend created by Buonarroti the poison of society in his own day.

Buonarroti transmits the traditions of the master : it is Babeuf with another name, Babeuf dying for a

---

[1] Édouard Fleury : *Babœuf et le Socialisme en 1796.* (1851.) The book ran into a second edition the following year.

second time in 1837, and born again in 1848 more
violent than ever—a fatal transmigration of souls, of
doctrines, of perversities !

Socialists, under whatever name—Egalitarians,
Fraternitarians, Icarians, Fourierists, Proudhonists—
socialists, to give them their generic name, have been
covered, exalted by Buonarroti. For us, it is still
Babeuf alive again in our own times. It is Babeuf
with a hundred heads. It is Babeuf who torments
our age more successfully than he tormented his own.
It is Babeuf from the grave revolutionizing society,
as he had failed to do while alive.

But it is Babeuf who will succumb again, under the
strong and invincible effort of society. He will win
from this frightful game only the sorry merit of once
again, in the person of his disciples, suffering martyrdom for the lost cause of an impossible and false
Equality.

It is obvious enough how absurdly exaggerated and
distorted this interpretation was. The bulk of Babeuf's
supporters were respectable and even prosperous mer-
chants, tradesmen and professional folk, and the last thing
most of them would have wanted was full-dress socialism.
Nor can the various schools of socialist thought be thus
cavalierly lumped together as the disciples of Babouvist
egalitarianism. But the reaction of Fleury and his followers was not rational. It was emotional, with a violence
equal to that of the extremists which alarmed him so
much. The notion of socialism as " Babeuf with a hundred
heads " was nevertheless widely accepted by conservative
opinion in the second half of the century. The conservative journals of 1851 gave Fleury's work a warm welcome.
Paul Janet, in 1880, contributed an article to the *Revue
des Deux Mondes* on eighteenth-century communism and

the Babeuf Plot which was largely inspired by, and based on, Fleury's work. In 1896 the Catholic social reformer Albert de Mun taunted Jules Guesde and his followers in the Chamber of Deputies with the cry : " Your origins lie in the Babeuf Plot and the Republic of Equals." " We accept that patronage ", retorted Guesde, and the next day reaffirmed his retort. " M. de Mun ", he said, " has fixed the cradle of the collectivist—or if you prefer communist—order, in the movement of the Equals and the Babeuf Plot : he has done so with our agreement and our applause."

In this way, the legend of Gracchus Babeuf, self-styled " Tribune of the People ", was not only fostered and nourished from within, by those who sympathized with his ideals of equality ; it went on being hardened and reinforced from without, by the attacks of those who saw in all socialistic movements the recurring nightmare of attacks on private property. The tactics of these conservative critics is a time-honoured one, and forms a strong cement for any legend of martyrdom. The English version of the same thing is Sir Robert Walpole insisting that all Tories were Jacobites in disguise, and we have become familiar in our own days with the " Red menace ", with all left-wingers being classed as " Bolshies ", and in return dubbing all right-wingers " Fascists ". We have it on the authority of Hitler that all enemies must be identified and presented as one single enemy before the masses can be inspired with confidence in revolutionary action. So Babeuf had importance and greatness thrust upon him from both sides.

The influence of Babouvism on the Republican Party of the Third Republic is tenuous for the reasons already mentioned. The tradition of the barricades and underground conspiracy had, after 1871, moved eastwards.

But no less a man than Arthur Ranc, friend and colleague of Léon Gambetta in the foundation of the Republican Party, saw fit to edit an abridged version of Buonarroti's book in 1869. And in his introduction to it he paid this homage :

> It is thanks to the Babouvists that, during the First Empire and the Restoration, the revolutionary tradition was never for a single instant broken, and that after the early days of 1830 the Republican Party reconstituted itself. They affirmed at the cost of their blood the urgent need for civilization to be founded exclusively on work and justice. At the same time intransigent revolutionaries, they never admitted that the social question and the political question could be for one moment separated. Finally, they persistently, indomitably and with invincible will marched towards their goal, which was the Republic—or in other words, Equality.

In the broad tradition of French Republicanism, perhaps the main importance of the legend of Babeuf is that it has helped to strengthen the awareness of Frenchmen that democracy is something to be defended and fought for—if need be behind the barricades. In England democracy is something legal and parliamentary—a civilian, constitutional order deeply rooted in the common law and slowly evolved parliamentary representative institutions. In the United States it is partly the ideal of a common life within an accepted electoral and federal system of government, partly the dream of a natural community of independent, self-reliant individuals comparable to a frontier society. In France, it is a burning sense of liberty and equality perpetually menaced by forces of reaction or subversion, the working of a " general will " which authority will ever frustrate if given the opportunity. Thus a moderate parliamentary Socialist like M. Louis Lévy can write a book to show that *France is a Democracy* (1943), in which the democratic and republican character of each region or locality in France is assessed by the degree of violent resistance it has shown to all attempts to overthrow the first three Republics. The temper and tempo of the democratic ideal in France, and of the Fourth Republic in particular, cannot be understood unless this peculiar republican tradition be grasped ; and the classical model of such last-ditch resistance is the Babeuf Plot.

For this reason, although the Babouvist legend and tradition inevitably tended to wither away once relative political stability was achieved in the Third French Republic, it still survived here and there in an attenuated form. It helps to explain, for example, French trade unions' preference for " direct action " rather than parliamentary politics. It had, after all, become an integral strand in the whole Republican tradition of struggle and resistance—and France was now a Republic. Nor was the Third Republic established without a decade of active struggle for survival ; this imprinted elements of Babouvism even on modern France. It imprinted them strongly enough for them to revive with full vigour after the Third Republic went down in national defeat in 1940, and republicanism again came to mean " resistance ".

The prolonged tussle between Monarchists and Republicans between 1871 and 1879 at first fortified Ranc's broad interpretation of the Republican tradition. From these years was born the modern Radical Party, the party of *nouvelles couches sociales* whose rise to power Gambetta foresaw and fostered after 1869. They have always, like Ranc, prided themselves in being the modern descendants of the direct Jacobin revolutionary tradition. They dominated the Third Republic. Though the party of peasant proprietors and small business men, they have clung to the political ideals of democratic republicanism without pursuing the social ideals of the revolutionary tradition. Their major battles have been won against Monarchy, Church and Army, and beyond this the immense social problems inherent in industrialism have been little tackled. For this reason, since 1879, when the "Republic of the Republicans" was finally secured, Radicalism has shed any Babouvist cult or associations.

But as after 1830 and 1848, other classes and parties were left unsatisfied, and even while adopting parliamentary methods the Socialists and Communists have clung to these social ideals left in abeyance by the Radicals. Under the Third Republic it was the parties of the Right —the Monarchists, Bonapartists and later the Fascists— which resorted to secret societies and subterranean agitation. The Babouvist traditions of secret conspiracy died out on the Left. The legend of Babouvism, diffused and weakened by the mere passing of time and change of circumstances, lingered on in only two ways : in the byways of politics and in the more flamboyant historical declarations of Left-wing party leaders.

The curious effect of Babouvist *mystique* on unbalanced or unlettered minds can be gauged from three pamphlets written by enthusiasts. A century ago a workman called Aloysius Huber gained some literary reputation for his two works on *L'Esclavage du riche* and the *Nuit de veille du prisonnier de l'État*. He reflected on the writings and ideas of Babeuf, Cabet and Louis Blanc and became obsessed with the need for " unity and association ". With the greatest excitement and naïveté he clamoured for more unity and closer human association as the cure for all poverty and distress. In 1931 appeared *Ressuscitons Babeuf : Essai sur le Programme Babouviste*, by Victor-Adolphe Bonthoux. It contained nothing about Babeuf's programme but only the personal egalitarian opinions of an old workman ; for the very good reason that the author admitted he had " never read a single line of Babeuf nor even a book about him ". Babeuf became a name to conjure with ; and perhaps the old French workman was merely being more honest in his admission than other more lettered minds which have at times felt impelled to pass judgment on Babeuf.

Jean Jaurès, after the manner of Guesde, claimed for Socialism direct descent from Babouvism. In his *Histoire Socialiste* he wrote :

> We are in an important sense—the sense in which Babeuf, following Robespierre, understood it—the party of democracy and of the Great Revolution. We do not intend to stabilize society in the economic formulae which prevailed from 1789 to 1794, and which correspond to living and working conditions that no longer exist.

The French Socialist Party, led by Jaurès, eagerly enough adopted Babeuf as a patron saint of their own movement. At the fourth Socialist Congress held at Tours in 1902, several members acclaimed the name of Babeuf. Gabriel Deville, who had already written a book in German about the Conspiracy, declared him to be undoubtedly *le premier socialiste conscient*. Jaurès, in a formal statement of party principles which he proposed and which was carried unanimously, declared :

> It was to extend to all citizens the guarantees inscribed in the Declaration of Rights that our great Babeuf demanded common property, as guarantee of the common happiness. For the bravest proletarians, communism was the supreme expression of the Revolution.

The eighth Socialist Party Congress, of 1911, was held at

Saint-Quentin, birthplace of Babeuf. It staged a solemn celebration in memory of the " great revolutionary ". Jaurès, in his *Histoire Socialiste de la Révolution Française*, credited Babeuf with foreseeing the historic role of the working classes in proletarian revolution.

> Babeuf found support especially among the factory workers. When he founded his club, it was at the Panthéon, at a point which was at the same time the centre of the Saint-Marcel quarter with its taverns and the Saint-Antoine quarter with its many powerful factories.

So, too, modern French Communists have claimed Babeuf as their own. M. Étienne Fajon has called him " the greatest of the forerunners of Communism in the Revolution of 1789 " and Communists have contrived to give their creed native roots, and even a tinge of nationalism in France, by adhering to this interpretation of the Conspiracy. Russian Communists have devoted close study to the whole affair since the Bolshevik Revolution. An abridged Russian version of Buonarroti's book appeared in Leningrad in 1923, and throughout the 1920's various books and articles on Babouvism and its significance for Marxism appeared from Russian presses ; but into the intricacies of Marxist exegesis it would be tedious to go.

It is a strange fate for the outcast of 1796 to have the great political parties of France jostling for a claim to hail him as an ancestor. He would have enjoyed it immensely, for he was never slow to assume greatness even when—as here—it was thrust upon him. One aspect, at least, of Babeuf's theory survives. All subsequent French history has endorsed the truth which he was among the first to state : that political liberty and equality, heralded by the Revolution of 1789, were unattainable without greater social and economic equality.   Of the two strands in the great revolutionary tradition, the political and the social, it was the first alone which won steady reeognition and success in the course of the nineteenth and early twentieth centuries.[1]   Only indeed in 1875 were the elementary political liberties of male suffrage, free elections and a free party-system achieved ;   only within the generation after that were the civic liberties of freedom of speech, the Press, public meeting and association fully secured ; only in 1945 was the vote extended to women.   But these political rights—just because they were so slowly and painfully attained—did not bring with them a corresponding advance in social or economic democracy.   There grew up a fateful divorce between the political and the social strands of the great Revolutionary tradition.

It may well be that the legend of Babouvism no less than Marxism helped to create this divorce.   Its scarifying associations and implications meant, in a land of peasant proprietorship and of expanding capitalist organization in industry and finance, that social reform of any kind was apt to be regarded as of the Devil.   Only in the generation after 1905, when the Dreyfus affair had worked itself out to a conclusion, Church had been separated from State, and the Republic securely established as a civilian, parliamentary régime, were social reforms seriously considered. In provision for social insurance, unemployment and poor relief, and the protection of industrial workers against exploitation, modern France has lagged behind England. Even in 1936 the belated " Popular Front " programme of social and economic reforms was regarded as revolutionary.

But in another sense, with the growing recognition in France that social and economic democracy must imple-

[1] The present author has elsewhere elaborated the distinction, and the significance of the distinction, between the political and the social implications of the ideals of 1789.   Cf. *Democracy in France : The Third Republic* (1946.)   Chap. I.

ment and supplement political democracy, Babouvism has in recent years come into its own. Each great political crisis of the Third Republic brought a more positive assertion of the need for social reform. It is significant that the main publications about Babeuf that have appeared in France have clustered around the periods of the Dreyfus case and the Popular Front experiment. At such moments Frenchmen have turned again to the potent republican legend of Babeuf. From time to time, since the days of 1796, the cry of " Bread and the Constitution of 1793 " has echoed down the Paris streets. It was often the aftermath of war. Its counterpart resounds in the world to-day, and not in France alone—again as the consequence of war. Whenever that happens, the gaunt shade of Gracchus Babeuf walks again. There is, indeed, *un Babouvisme de nos jours.*

CHAPTER IV

LE BABOUVISME DE NOS JOURS

THE peculiarly French sense that not only is eternal vigilance the price of liberty, but also that violence is the ultimate sanction of democracy, is born of France's whole history. The tradition of Babouvism is but one strand in this long history. It is significant that the nearest English equivalent to the Babouvists—the Levellers and Diggers of the seventeenth century—date from the era when England bore the reputation for political fickleness and instability that France has acquired since 1789. It would seem that doctrinaire egalitarianism goes hand in hand with a revolutionary tradition. It is in a sense an eccentricity born of social upheaval. As such, it is smothered when the period of social upheaval comes to an end. It survived as an indigenous movement in France chiefly because the great Revolution was followed by a century of political upheavals, each arousing fresh hopes in the leading disciples of Babouvism—Buonarroti and Blanqui, and their followers.

The nearest modern English counterpart to the French egalitarians is Mr. George Bernard Shaw. For him Socialism has always meant, fundamentally, equality of incomes. In his latest political work *Everybody's Political What's What* (1944), he writes :

> The statesman aiming at equal distribution of income will find that he must fix a wage figure at which no talent or genius can be wasted through lack of the means for its fullest cultivation. As this figure will at first exceed that arrived at by dividing the

89

total national income by the number of people in the country, he must maintain the incomes of the bureaucracy and the professions at the fixed figure as a first charge on the national income. The rest he must distribute as best he can with equality of income as his goal, using every device to increase the national income and using the increase to level up the lowest wage to the grade above it until all the grades are levelled up to the fixed figure, and equality of income attained, virtually if not mathematically.

In England, in short, Mr. Shaw is the exception that proves the rule : the eccentricity of Mr. Shaw's genius does not need a social upheaval to produce it, and the contrast between Babouvist and Fabian methods of pursuing the goal of equality is eloquent comment on the difference between the course of French and of British democratic development in modern times.

Indeed the ideal of equality, which in the present century has come to play an increasingly active part in the democratic ideal, has—for historical reasons—a different connotation in each of the major democratic countries. " The conception of Equality ", wrote Lord Bryce at the end of the first world war, " has been the prime factor in the creation of democratic theory, and from misunderstandings of it have sprung half the errors which democratic practice has committed." Even so profound a student of democracy could add, at so late a date, that " Democracy—which is merely a form of government, not a consideration of the purposes to which government may be turned—has nothing to do with Economic Equality, which might exist under any form of government, and might possibly work more smoothly under some other form". Until the twentieth century the ideal of equality, whilst meaning something different in each country, was in none generally regarded as involving economic equality. There are therefore three outstanding questions to be considered before the precise meaning of equality in modern France can be determined. How did French democratic ideals differ from those of other countries (especially Britain and the United States) before the conception of economic equality intruded into all of them ? What differences of emphasis in interpretation of the ideal of economic equality have arisen in each country ? And finally, what consequences and significance have both these sets of differences for the understanding of republicanism in France ?

The essence of democracy, which distinguishes it sharply from all totalitarianisms, is respect for human personality. The democratic ideal rests on the belief that the individual human being, just because he is human, must be the test of all political, legal and social arrangements. The State must exist for man, not man for the State : so too must the legal order and the social order. Logically, then, the conception of equality is no less vital to its fulfilment than the conception of liberty ; and historically these were twin ideals. The only basis on which the plea for man's liberty can rest is the belief that all men should be equally free. Liberty for some men at the price of slavery for other men is not liberty as modern democrats have conceived it. The ancient Athenian citizen partially founded his own liberty on slavery ; but no modern democrat would be satisfied with such liberty. Liberty, for him, presupposes that belief in the ultimate common humanity of men which democrats have learnt to call " equality " : the only basis on which the plea for man's liberty can rest in the simultaneous plea that all men should be equally free.

In the seventeenth and eighteenth centuries democrats in England, America and France alike emphasized this intimate connection between the ideals of liberty and equality. In the Putney Debates between the Puritan leaders of 1647, Colonel Rainboro made the famous passionate declaration : " Really, I think the poorest he that is in England hath a life to live as the richest he." In 1776 the American Declaration of Independence followed the same logic :

> We hold these truths to be self-evident : that all men are created equal ; that they are endowed by their Creator with inalienable rights ; that among these rights are life, liberty, and the pursuit of happiness.

Thirteen years later the French Revolutionaries repeated the creed :

> Men are born and remain free and equal in rights.

Both ideals linked closely on to the third element in the French Revolutionary slogan : Fraternity. As Robert Burns put it, " a man's a man for a' that ".

But underneath this surface unity of aims of all eighteenth-century democrats lay an important difference of emphasis. The democratic ideal had two roots : Christian and humanist ; theological and rationalist. It was one thing to maintain, like the Puritans, that every man has a soul and that all human souls are of equal value in the eyes of God ; and another thing to insist, like the English common lawyers, that all men are citizens and therefore equal in the eyes of the law. It was one thing to believe, like Luther, in the " priesthood of all believers ", and the equal right of access of all, through faith, to Divine Grace ; and another thing to believe, like Bentham, in the equal right of all men, by reason of their common humanity, to an equal share of happiness. In the course of historical development these different currents of democratic faith tended to intermingle and frequently to work in practice in the same direction. But the fundamental disparity between their origins and nature produced different effects in each country, according to how and in what proportions they intermingled.

In England the growth of legal equality and the growth of religious equality were intimately connected. The conception of religious equality as an ideal preceded in time the achievement of legal equality ; but this, in turn, substantially preceded the achievement of religious equality. The triumph of the common law in the seventeenth century coincided with the flight of Puritans from persecution and the failure of their claim to religious freedom and equality. Toleration of dissent came only slowly and gradually during the eighteenth century, partly because it was a period of steady consolidation and definition of the common law ; but political and civil disabilities of Dissenters were finally removed only after the nineteenth century had run more than half its course. There followed closely the achievement of political democracy—the evolution and elaboration of the parliamentary representative system, the principle of one man one vote, freedom of speech, the Press, public meetings and association, and eventually—though only in the twentieth century—the emancipation of women and the principle of equality between the sexes.

It was a peculiar characteristic of the growth of British ideas of democracy that the religious and the secular notions of liberty and equality were never far apart. The constant determining factor was the co-existence, within one island community, of diverse religious bodies. After the Civil War the acceptance of toleration as inevitable gradually became the keynote of British politics. In 1687 the Catholic King of England, James II, issued a Declaration of Indulgence suspending penal laws in ecclesiastical affairs ; two years before the Catholic King of France, Louis XIV, had revoked the Edict of Nantes and so out-lawed his Protestant subjects. James paid for such acts with his throne, Louis paid for them with the economic well-being of the country. But whereas John Locke, the official theorist and apologist of the Whig Revolution which forced James to abdicate, was himself a champion of toleration, the rigid orthodoxy of the French monarchy led to the scepticism and anti-clericalism of Voltaire. Freedom of worship became in England the bedrock of civil and political freedom ; something already achieved was the solid foundation of further achievement. Freedom of criticism became in France the prime demand of the *philosophes*, whose attitude to the Church was summarized in the slogan *écrasez l'infâme* ![1]

Because, in France, the Catholic Church was so closely identified historically with the Monarchy, and because, in time of revolutionary crisis, it chose so closely to identify itself with the *ancien régime*, the demand for the abolition of feudal privileges inevitably became an attack on the Church itself. The power and iniquity of the priestcraft became a favourite theme of the rationalists. As Babeuf discovered to his cost, there was little difference, in prac-tice, between the attitude of the higher clergy and the attitude of the secular nobility towards the middle classes. The obstacle to liberty, equality, democracy, happiness and progress—all now coming to be treated as kindred aims—was primarily legal and social privilege. Because Church and Monarchy were part and parcel of this net-work of privilege called the *ancien régime*, it was inevitable that these aims should come to be inseparable from secularism and republicanism. Already, to more vivid

---

[1] Cf. W. G. Addison : *Religious Equality in Modern England, 1714–1914.* (1944.) Kingsley Martin : *French Liberal Thought in the Eighteenth Century.* (1929.)

imaginations, the vision of the last King strangled with the entrails of the last priest was the only imaginable prelude to the reign of reason and democracy. *L'infâme* was not merely the Church—it was all superstition and all intolerance. And when intolerance had been paradoxically " crushed " so intolerantly, the kind of " toleration " that emerged could scarcely be the same as that which Englishmen had experienced under the placid rule of a Robert Walpole or a Henry Pelham. It would be as different as was the French Revolution of 1789 from the English Revolution of a century before.

In these ways, whilst the religiously and politically tolerant society of eighteenth-century England was producing a parliamentary system of democracy in which civil liberties were valued more than egalitarianism, the religiously and politically intolerant society of eighteenth-century France was giving birth to a doctrine and conception of democracy in which equality—in the sense of absence of legal and social privilege—was valued above parliamentary institutions of which France had virtually no experience, and above civil or personal freedom which seemed likely to follow, and not precede, the achievement of equality. Liberty and equality in England became ideals partially embodied in familiar and deep-rooted institutions, such as Parliament and the Common Law, whose pursuit could therefore be carried out by gradual reform and legislative change. In France they became more rigid doctrines, closely knit with rationalist philosophy, which were at complete variance with all that the existing order stood for and which could be achieved only by drastic overhaul of that old order. In England religious and legal equality, hard-won by civil war and consolidated by nearly a century of tolerant oligarchic rule, could serve as the foundation for political and civil equality. These achieved, social and economic equality lost their potency as operative ideals. In France, legal and social equality were achieved simultaneously in the Revolution, and even a limited kind of economic equality was achieved too, in the sense that financial privilege and exemptions from taxation were abolished and a large degree of economic independence was attained by the increase of peasant proprietorship. But these gains were made at the expense, so to speak, of political equality. Republicanism remained, especially after the reverses of 1804–71, on the defensive—having to fight for survival against Bonapartists and Monarchists and Communards, it remained a belligerent creed—and in spirit and teaching it was therefore forced to be intolerant of all political rivals. It is no accident that French Republicans had to talk so much, so often and so loudly about the doctrines of liberty and equality—in Declarations of the Rights of Man, in paper-constitutions and in political manifestos : nor that distinctions between " active " and " passive " citizens, property and sex qualifications for the vote, and violent conflicts between " Right " and " Left ", abound in French political history and philosophy since 1789.

From this contrast of development between France and England there springs, too, a most important contrast between two different conceptions of economic equality. Equality of wealth can be sought by two diverse methods : by distributivism—" three acres and a cow " for every peasant, and a chicken in every pot ; or by communal ownership of all means of production, and distribution of wealth according to needs. At the very time when France was going so far towards achieving the first kind of economic equality among her peasantry, England was destroying the last shreds of her yeomanry by enclosures and by the growth of urban industrialism. When, in sixteenth-century England, the lands of the monasteries had been distributed, they went to the wealthier land-owners and the new gentry, and so created a vested interest against the Counter-Reformation. When, in eighteenth-century France, the lands of Church and nobles were divided, they went to the middle classes and the peasants, and so created a vested interest against the Restoration. Likewise nineteenth-century Liberalism in both countries meant free ownership of property, freedom of enterprise and economic independence, but because of the different balance of social forces the movement produced different effects. In England, Liberalism meant freedom of enterprise for the trader and the industrialist, and involved an attack on the privileges of the landed and agricultural interest. In France, it meant also freedom of enterprise for the trader and the industrialist, but it meant, too, freedom of enterprise for the peasant farmer and involved no essential attack on agrarian interests. Only in the later nineteenth and the twentieth centuries was there any open and significant conflict between the interests of agriculturists and industrialists (whether employers or workers), because only then did French industry become important enough and integrated enough to challenge seriously the various benefits and advantages acquired by agricultural interests.

This further contrast had important consequences for the spirit and structure of organized labour in both countries. The English trade unions and other labour or co-operative movements grew up in tune with—and in some ways as part of—the liberal and parliamentary tradition. They demanded equality of rights with other associations (like the Free Churches) and sought their ends eventually by familiar parliamentary and political methods : their aim was legal protection, freedom of collective bargaining, and freedom of association. French trade unions grew up in hostility to the French liberal

E

tradition, which was so closely identified with business interests on one hand and with the interests of peasant proprietors on the other. They were more syndicalist, collectivist and even communistic than they were liberal ; their demands were for freedom of direct action, for special powers within the community rather than for equality of treatment with other associations ; their conception of economic equality was collectivist rather than distributivist. They wanted " National workshops " rather than Workmen's Compensation Acts, a " Workers' Republic " rather than a place within a parliamentary constitution ; and they therefore quite logically eschewed parliamentary party-politics and adhered to a policy of direct action through strike, boycott and sabotage. In short, the peculiar tradition of the barricades found natural continuity within the movements of organized labour ; and it is not surprising that the trade unions became, during German occupation between 1940 and 1945, the source of sustained and well-organized resistance.

This broad contrast—which would have to be modified somewhat for the attitude of trade unions since liberation —helps to explain the peculiar shade of meaning implied by the ideal of economic equality in France, and the special place of Babouvism in the context of French political life and thought. It explains, for example, something of that gulf between French Radicalism and French Socialism, which has no real counterpart in England. English Radicalism is inherent in the English trade-union movement : French Radicalism, standing for the distributivist conception of economic equality, is sharply divided from French Socialism, which stands predominantly for the collectivist conception of equality. It is the modern equivalent to that gulf between Jacobins and Babouvists in 1796 ; and behind it lies the long story of violent controversy and conflict between those who saw in Socialism

" Babeuf with a hundred heads " and those who looked back to the Babeuf Plot as the first practical attempt to achieve economic equality through communist organization of society. It also explains why Babouvism, apart from the brief adoption of it by the ill-fated Chartist movement of the " hungry forties ", has remained so little studied and so generally unappreciated in England.

Meanwhile, an even more striking and dramatic series of contrasts in development had been taking place in the United States of America. From seventeenth and eighteenth-century England, America had inherited the Puritan tradition, the institutions and ways of thought of the common law, and the ideal of toleration. Taking these elements, the course of American history changed and combined them in striking new ways with important new consequences both for America and for the world. To them she added a conception of democratic freedom and equality derived from her own frontier spirit, which had in many respects closer affiliations with the French ideals of economic independence through peasant proprietorship than with anything in English life. To generations of American citizens in the nineteenth century, and to great leaders like Thomas Jefferson and Andrew Jackson, democratic society came to be visualized in terms of frontier communities, where the welfare, happiness and freedom of each citizen depended on " mixing his labour " with his own land, on vigorous self-help and enterprise. The distributivist ideal of equality held the field. Just as in France *la carrière ouverte aux talents* became the most highly prized residue of the Revolutionary and Napoleonic achievements, so in America grew up a society wherein the road " from log-cabin to White House " in political life, and from cabin-boy to multi-millionaire in economic life, became the focus of the American dream. " Equality of opportunity ", in a rapidly expanding community, swamped all other conceptions of equality ; and that, of course, could have nothing to do with economic equality in any collectivist sense. Again, it is no accident that labour movements and trade-union organizations have been peculiarly slow to develop in the United States, or that social services and provision for " social security " have little concerned American opinion until the experience of twentieth-century industrialism—and of twentieth-century slumps—raised them as acutely urgent problems. Despite the strong historical links and sentimental sympathies between France and America—at two crucial stages in their history both countries found themselves allied against Britain—it is not surprising that Babouvism has attracted even less attention in America than in Britain. The distance can be measured by the differences of spirit and programme between the " Popular Front " Government of 1936 and the " New Deal " of President Roosevelt, each devised to meet the needs of the economic depression and fascist threats of the mid-nineteen-thirties : a reliable gauge of the temper and character of a nation's democratic ideals, equalled only by the test of war itself to which both countries submitted a few years later.

Mr. J. B. Priestley has expressed the American's dilemma well.

> His very slang gives him away. He does not want to stick his neck out, he wants to go along with the gang, he wants to be a regular fellow. These do not suggest a passionate concern about liberty, but they do suggest that equality is all-important. A regular fellow is equal to other regular fellows. The dream is tethered, a huge dim captive balloon, to that historic phrase about men being created equal. But this is not the eighteenth century, and the United

States no longer consists of struggling rural communities sending pioneers into a vast wilderness. . . .
If we are now largely governed by our economic life
—and one need not be a Marxist to admit that—then
to dream of equality, yet to leave economic life so
uncontrolled that it produces the gravest inequalities,
is to ask for frustration.   And this, of course, is the
American dilemma.   America makes use of its old
revolution to block all possible new ones.   Because it
had one once, there need not be another.[1]

It is, in short, legal and social equality in the sense that
eighteenth-century France cherished the ideals—the absence of formal and artificial impediments to self-realiza-
tion—that Americans most value.   Relative unconcern
for political equality is shown by the lateness of female
suffrage in the Union (1920) and by the fact that negroes
are still, in many parts of the Union, effectively prevented
from exercising the vote and from holding political or
civil office.   Complete unconcern for economic equality
is evident in every stratum of American life, from the
homage paid to high-paid film stars and multi-million-
aires, to the acquiescence of the poor whites and the
ill-paid farm labourer.   Though much has changed in
the last generation, and much more will change in the
next, it remains substantially true that liberty and equality
of opportunity loom largest in the American vision of
democracy.   It was the greatest of modern Americans
who spoke so eloquently of " the Four Freedoms " as the
essence of America's war aims

The other side of the coin may be illuminated by comparison with developments in the other of the modern
" Big Four " Powers—Soviet Russia.   Whereas Babouv-

[1] J. B. Priestley : *The Secret Dream.* (1946.) Chap. III on " America
and Equality ".

ism has been completely neglected in the United States, and barely noticed in Britain, it has been studied almost as closely in Soviet Russia as in France itself. The reason is not far to seek ; and it does not lie merely in that affiliation with Marxist ideology already discussed. In 1917 Russia stood at the parting of the ways between the two broad kinds of economic equality. Lenin's cry after the March Revolution was " All land to the peasants ". The Provisional Government established after the March Revolution had, indeed, been trying to conduct both foreign war and social revolution at the same time ; but attempts to distribute lands to the peasants had led to the virtual dissolution of the Russian armies, because so many of the peasant-soldiers returned home to claim their share. The distributivist ideals of the Provisional Government and the apparent distributivism of Lenin's slogan were both short-lived. They were quickly followed by an over-hasty attempt at collectivism—the requisitioning by the State of all supplies, and the abolition of " private profit ". And this, in turn, had to give way to the compromise period of Lenin's " New Economic Policy ". More gradually collective farms were established, modest peasant proprietorship was allowed while the wealthy *kulaks* were eliminated. At the same time, the whole balance of economic production and of social life was altered by the planned industrialization of the Five-Year Plans. The distributivist ideal of economic equality was completely replaced by the collectivist. But this, in turn, gave rise to a further dilemma. Was the principle of distribution of communally owned and collectively pro-duced wealth to be " to each according to his work " ? Or was it to be " to each according to his needs " ?[1] The former was eventually adopted as the principle of the

---

[1] It was the dilemma already recognized, in French political thought, by the difference between Saint-Simon and Louis Blanc. Cf. p. 70 above.

first stage of collectivism—" Socialism " ; the second as the further stage of more complete collectivism—" Communism ". Neither is rigidly egalitarian nor is Marxist ideology in itself egalitarian. The abolition of "unearned income " is its prime concern ; inequalities of earned income are regarded as inevitable and in many respects just. This whole evolution naturally aroused interest in the early form of communistic equality associated with the Babeuf Plot ; though, as already shown, this has been officially regarded by Marxists as a primitive, premature and in many ways wrong-headed version of communism.

Clearly enough the broad effect of the Communist experiment has been a levelling. The gulf between very rich and very poor has been narrowed. As in other countries, the extension of social services provided by the State or its subsidiary agencies, and paid for by either State ownership of the means of production or by steeply graded taxation and heavy death-duties, has been mainly responsible for this levelling. Social services are paid for ultimately " according to capacity ", and are normally distributed " according to need ". With such machinery in operation, providing a wide variety of amenities for the poorest and a higher degree of social security for all against old age, illness, death, and other misfortunes, the notion of rigid economic equality loses its attractions.

The closest affinity that this levelling tendency of Marxism has with egalitarianism à la française is that both are rooted in secular, rationalist and even materialist philosophy, and neither derives in any considerable measure from Christian or religious concepts of human equality. This, more than anything else, helps to explain the relative rigidity and intolerance of both creeds as compared with egalitarianism in Britain or America, where the traditions of Puritanism and the Free Churches have done so much to offset absolutist doctrines and to moderate intolerance. One example may suffice : the development of a national system of education. In Britain and America freedom of education, distrust of orthodoxy, affection for variety and heterogeneity, have dominated ideas on education. Full respect has been paid, even in State-run schools and universities, to non-conformity whether religious or merely political. In France and Russia the dominant political parties—though vastly different in each case—have sought to impose, and have largely succeeded in creating, an educational system that is highly integrated. Each is designed as the vehicle for a positive philosophy to be inculcated in the rising generation of its citizens. And in each case this has been achieved primarily in the name of equality.

Within the educational framework founded by Napoleon as a buttress of unified control, the Radicals of the Third Republic established a national system of instruction which was anti-clerical in spirit, nationalistic in purport, and remarkably uniform in shape. The leading figure in this development was Jules Ferry, a Radical inspired by the ideals of eighteenth-century French Republicanism. The conviction of Republicans that the Republic would not be safe and could not be " democratic " until laicism prevailed in national education sprang from the century-old battle between Church and State : born of battle, the French educational system was infused with a harsh, intolerant spirit unknown in British or American education. Equality of citizenship, social and political equality, were regarded as depending on the exclusion of the Church from the schools, and of religious teaching from the syllabus. The fear of every good Republican was restoration—return to the privileged, hierarchical order of the *ancien régime*. Education of the masses therefore became the favourite inoculation against royalism, clericalism and privilege.

So in Russia the onslaught on illiteracy, ignorance and superstition which the Bolshevik régime prepared was combined with an attack on the power of the Church and the privileges of the old Tsarist aristocracy and official-dom. Lenin would have agreed with the dictum of Napoleon : " As long as children are not taught whether they ought to be Republican or Monarchist, Catholic or irreligious, the State will not form a Nation ". As a precaution of political hygiene, certain orthodox beliefs had to be inculcated : children must be taught not merely how to think, but what to think. And in Russia the central justification was a levelling up—the provision for all citizens of facilities which had hitherto been the exclusive privilege of the well-to-do. One recalls Babeuf's contention that education should be either provided equally for all or withheld equally from all ; his only error was to imagine that these are alternative and mutually exclusive achievements.

Le Babouvisme de nos jours has, then, these chief characteristics : as a levelling movement, fired by the need to diminish and bridge the gulf between rich and poor, and to ensure a tolerable minimum standard of well-being and wealth for every citizen, its achievements have become merged into the structure and ideals of the social-service State ; as a movement of more doctrinaire egalitarianism, it has retained something of its original fervour only in its country of origin, France. In Great Britain, and to a greater extent in the United States, the collectivist and anti-liberal elements of egalitarianism have been tempered and offset by the traditions of liberalism, of the Free Churches, toleration, and freedom of association. In Russia, the collectivist conception of equality has triumphed, although inequalities of earned income are tolerated and even encouraged. Historically Babouvism was an early, violent reaction against the social divisions and economic distress of the modern world, made at a dramatic moment of European history. The answer it offered to these problems was crude, doctrinaire and in itself inadequate ; but the moment of its appearance ensured it permanent attention. And perhaps its greatest triumph is very recent—in the French " Resistance Charter " of 1944 and the Constitution of the Fourth Republic of 1946.

All the major parties of the Fourth French Republic went to the polls in October 1945, pledged to support the general programme set forth in the " Resistance Charter ". It had been drawn up in March 1944 as an expression of the aims of the organized resistance movements in their fight for liberation from German rule. It places social security and economic reforms in the forefront of modern French politics. When it speaks of the desire for " a true economic and social democracy ", for " an economy which will assure the subordination of private interests to the common interest ", and for " ensuring for all citizens the means of subsistence in all cases where they cannot earn their own living ", it is paying the latest homage to the traditions of French socialistic thought and idealism which began with Babeuf. With varying degrees of emphasis but in real concord, the leading parties of the Fourth Republic have based their policies on the assumptions that political, social and economic democracy are inseparable ideals, none of which can be achieved without simultaneous effort to achieve the others. This agreement has found embodiment in the Constitution of the Fourth Republic, accepted by popular referendum in October 1946. Its preamble reaffirms certain " political, economic and social principles particularly necessary in our time "; and these are the principles of the Resistance Charter. The Fourth Republic fittingly marks the climax of the Republican legend which Babeuf began 150 years ago.

A NOTE ON AUTHORITIES

IT has been thought advisable not to impede the story by a flutter of footnotes and references to authorities ; but as the sources of information about Babeuf and his followers are complex, a few remarks about sources and authorities may usefully be added.

The original materials for the history of Babeuf and the Plot, other than Babeuf's own published writings in book or journal form, are scattered among the Marx-Engels-Lenin Institute in Moscow, the *Bibliothèque Nationale* and *Archives Nationales* in Paris, and various local and municipal archives in France. Fortunately all the main documentary sources have, however, been printed in two main works : these are Philippe Buonarroti's important work mentioned in the text (*Conspiration pour l'égalité dite de Babeuf, suivie du procès auquel elle donna lieu, et des pièces justicatives*, etc. 2 Volumes, 1828) and Victor Advielle's patient compilation (*Histoire de Gracchus Babeuf et du babouvisme, d'après de nombreux documents inédits.* 2 Volumes, 1884). These two works remain the basic published authorities for any student of Babeuf. To them must be added the official *Débats des Procès* . . ., published in four volumes in 1797 : the full report of the trial of the conspirators.

Much piecemeal research, however, has subsequently been done which has corrected or amplified many of the details there provided. The chief of these in French are as follow :

Espinas, Alfred. *La Philosophie sociale du XVIIIe siècle et la Révolution.* (1898.) Espinas did for Babouvism at the end of the century what Buonarroti did for it at the beginning—he restated it in terms of later experience ; some 200 pages of the book are devoted to Babeuf.
Thibout, Georges. *La doctrine babouviste.* (1903.) An academic and scholarly analysis of Babeuf's theories.

Robiquet, Paul. *Buonarroti et la secte des Égaux d'après des documents inédits.* (1910.) It is based on Buonarroti's papers, and sheds much light on the early phases of the legend.

Patoux, Abel. *Le faux de Gracchus Babeuf.* (1913.) A detailed study of the charges of forgery brought against Babeuf in 1793.

Dommanget, Maurice. *Babeuf et la conjuration des Égaux.* (1922.) Probably the best and most balanced account of the life of Babeuf, the Plot and the subsequent legend. The same author has published also :

Pages Choisies de Babeuf. (1935.) As well as providing a most useful anthology of Babeuf's writings for the general student, he here corrects and elaborates in his notes some of the points made in the earlier book. He also provides an admirable bibliography.

Walter, Gerald. *Babeuf et le Babouvisme.* (1933.) A detailed and cautiously sceptical account and interpretation of the historical importance of Babeuf.

Montgrenier, René. *Gracchus Babeuf.* (1937.)

Haenisch, Walter. *La Vie et les Lettres de Philippe Buonarroti.* (1938.)

In addition, many useful articles have appeared in various journals dealing with particular parts of Babeuf's life or of his ideas. The most important of these are :

Deville, Gabriel. *Notes inédites de Babeuf sur lui-même. La Révolution française.* Vol. XLIX. (1905.)

Janet, Paul. *Les origines du socialisme contemporain :* II. *Le communisme au XVIIIe, siècle et la conspiration de Babeuf. Revue des Deux Mondes.* Vol. XL. (1880.)

Mathiez, Albert. *Le Directoire. Babeuf et le Directoire. Le complot des Égaux. La politique de ralliement et l'affaire de Grenelle. Revue des Cours et Conférences.* (1929.) Nos. 11, 13, 14, 15, 16.

Robiquet, Paul. *Babeuf et Barras. La Revue de Paris.* (1896.)

Thomas, Albert. *La pensée socialiste de Babeuf avant la conspiration des Égaux. La Revue Socialiste.* (1904–5.)

Weill, Georges. *Philippe Buonarroti. Les papiers de Buonarroti, Revue Historique.* (1901 and 1905.)

The standard of scholarship applied to all the above studies is high. But there is a mass of partisan writing on the subject of which only the three most important examples may be mentioned. These are :

Fleury, Edouard. *Babœuf et le socialisme en 1796.* (1851.) Violently antagonistic in spirit, yet scholarly enough to merit attention, and important as founding the anti-Babeuf tradition of conservative history.

Méric, Victor. *Gracchus Babeuf.* (1907.) An equally violent partisan apologia by a man who was himself an active social revolutionary.

Ehrenberg, Ilya. *La Vie de Gracchus Babeuf.* (1929.) A hasty and unhistorical essay by the well-known modern Russian publicist.

In English there is very little. The main work is :

Bax, E. B. *The Last Episode of the French Revolution.* (1911.) A readable but often slipshod writing-up of the early authorities.

There is a brief and superficial essay on Babeuf in :

Whitham, J. Mills. *French Revolutionary Historical and Biographical Studies.* (1933.)

The place of Babouvism in political thought is assessed in most general books about political theory, and especially about Socialist theory. Of these the best are—in French :

Weill, Georges. *Le Parti républicain en France, 1814–1810.* (1900.)

Tchernoff, I. A. *Le Parti républicain sous la Monarchie de Juillet.* (1901.) *Associations et Sociétés secrètes sous la Deuxième République.* (1905.) *Le Parti républicain . . . sous le Second Empire.* (1906.)

Prudhommeaux, Jules. *Étienne Cabet et les Origines du Communisme Icarien.* (1907.)

And in English :

Laidler, H. W.   *A History of Socialist Thought.*   (1927.)
Martin, K. B.   *French Liberal Thought in the Eighteenth Century.*
    (1929.)
Soltau, R.   *French Political Thought in the Nineteenth Century.*
    (1931.)
Gray, A.   *The Socialist Tradition : Moses to Lenin.*   (1946.)

INDEX